ENGAGING CHINA

Myth, Aspiration, and Strategy in Canadian Policy
from Trudeau to Harper

"Engagement" has been the bedrock of Canada's policy toward China for more than four decades. Ottawa has continually attempted to assist China's entry into the international system and to advance a commercial agenda. Yet engagement has also been conceived by many Canadians in larger terms as a moral enterprise intended to influence or change China's domestic social and political order. As China's economic and diplomatic reach has expanded, policy makers in Ottawa have struggled to devise a compelling strategy that addresses the rise of global China and the mixture of anxiety and opportunity this has generated in Canadian minds.

Engaging China is a concise account of the evolution and current state of Canada's policy toward China – its achievements, failings, and dilemmas. Written by Paul Evans, one of Canada's foremost experts on contemporary Asian affairs, the volume inaugurates the UTP Insights series of books that take on the issues crucial to understanding our world and Canada's place within it. Evans's assessment of Canada's China policy speaks to the idea of engagement, its intellectual history, and its contradictions and possibilities.

Clearly presented and cogently argued, *Engaging China* outlines the elements necessary for a comprehensive and strategic approach to China in light of its central role in the most important power shift in the global order since the Second World War.

PAUL M. EVANS teaches contemporary Asia-Pacific affairs at the University of British Columbia.

UTP Insights

UTP Insights is an innovative collection of brief books offering accessible introductions to the issues that shape our world. Each volume in the series focuses on a contemporary issue, offering a fresh perspective anchored in contemporary scholarship. Spanning a broad range of disciplines in the social sciences and humanities, the books in the UTP Insights series will set the agenda for public discourse and debate, as well as provide valuable resources for students and instructors.

BOOKS IN THE SERIES

- Paul M. Evans, *Engaging China: Myth, Aspiration, and Strategy in Canadian Policy from Trudeau to Harper*

ENGAGING CHINA

Myth, Aspiration, and Strategy in Canadian Policy from Trudeau to Harper

Paul M. Evans

UNIVERSITY OF TORONTO PRESS
Toronto Buffalo London

© University of Toronto Press
Toronto Buffalo London
www.utppublishing.com
Printed in Canada

ISBN 978-1-4426-4655-1 (cloth)
ISBN 978-1-4426-1448-2 (paper)

Printed on acid-free, 100% post-consumer recycled paper with vegetable-based inks

---

Library and Archives Canada Cataloguing in Publication

Evans, Paul M., author
Engaging China : myth, aspiration, and strategy in Canadian policy
from Trudeau to Harper / Paul Evans.

(UTP insights)
Includes bibliographical references and index.
ISBN 978-1-4426-4655-1 (bound). – ISBN 978-1-4426-1448-2 (pbk.)

1. Canada – Foreign relations – China – History – 20th century.   2. Canada – Foreign relations – China – History – 21st century.   3. China – Foreign relations – Canada – History – 20th century.   4. China – Foreign relations – Canada – History – 21st century.   I. Title.   II. Series: UTP insights.

FC251.C5E95 2014   327.71051   C2013-908760-5

University of Toronto Press acknowledges the financial assistance to its publishing program of the Canada Council for the Arts and the Ontario Arts Council.

Canada Council   Conseil des Arts
for the Arts   du Canada

ONTARIO ARTS COUNCIL
CONSEIL DES ARTS DE L'ONTARIO
50 YEARS OF ONTARIO GOVERNMENT SUPPORT OF THE ARTS
50 ANS DE SOUTIEN DU GOUVERNEMENT DE L'ONTARIO AUX ARTS

University of Toronto Press acknowledges the financial support of the Government of Canada through the Canada Book Fund for its publishing activities.

To the thought leaders of our era searching for a morally compelling, politically sustainable, and mutually advantageous approach to China that creatively connects Canadian values, identity, and interests to an ascending China charting an uncertain path in a messy, multicentric world order.

For Catherine, tolerant, inspiring, and ever loving, and in memory of Thomas J. Delworth, who never really liked China but felt we could find a good way to live with it.

The time is past when China or "the Chinese" can properly be the object simply of our curiosity, our philanthropy, or our fear. Living with them in one world is going to be serious business, demanding study and effort on our part, not least because the tables have turned and we now seem to them out of date, backward, lacking in moral self-discipline and addicted to the evils of affluent waste, individual license, and public violence that mankind can no longer afford to tolerate. At the same time, however, China's future is not ours. Neither our circumstances nor our traditions compel us toward their degree of collectivism and crowded living. Conflict and misunderstanding between us can be mitigated roughly in proportion as [we see ourselves] and each other in realistic historical perspective.

John K. Fairbank, "Power Politics: Concepts and Misconceptions, 1898–1972," in *Chinese American Interactions: A Historical Summary*, 1975, 78–9

Contents

Preface

Today's overriding strategic question in capitals around the world is how to respond to the rise of Asia as a centre of gravity in world affairs and in particular the fourth rise of China as a major global player. China was the largest economy in the world until the mid-nineteenth century and very likely will be so again soon. Contemporary China is not exotic, distant, or insular but rather integrated into the world economy and a global force in diplomatic, military, and economic terms. The choices of the Chinese government, Chinese business leaders, and Chinese consumers have impact virtually everywhere. It is difficult to think of a single global issue—climate change, cyber security, pandemics, water usage, non-proliferation—where the path to solutions does not run through Beijing as well as Washington.

A legion of sceptics believe that China's rise is coming to an end, that it lacks the economic fundamentals and political institutions to sustain growth and stability, that it is on the verge of an implosion generated by internal social protest, and that it is headed for destructive conflict with the United States and its Asian neighbours. They are as much afraid of China as afraid for China.

I begin from a different starting point. The real challenge is not Chinese weakness but growing Chinese power at a moment when an American-centred international system is being supplanted by a multipolar—more precisely a multicentric—balance of world power. China's resumption of power and influence is one of the transformative developments of this century. Its economic power is not just as a manufacturer; it is as a buyer, seller, investor, development assistance

provider, recipient and source of foreign direct investment, global financier, and innovator. Its political power is that it is becoming a rule
maker, and occasional rule breaker, with a major hand in defining the
rules, norms, and institutions of global order in ways that only two
decades ago seemed unimaginable.

Ideas about a "G-2 world," "two suns in the sky," and a "Beijing
consensus" as an authoritarian alternative to Western democracy
and capitalism misrepresent what is happening. But even if exag-
gerated and inflammatory, they reflect the insight that the world order is undergoing its most significant realignment since the Second
World War.

The China challenge is much bigger than the Japan challenge of
the 1980s because of the difference in scale; it is more threatening
and complicated than the Soviet challenge of the Cold War because
Chinese power is more comprehensive, because China is a much
more integrated part of a global capitalist system, and because
China is propelled by specific national interests and historical images rather than ideology.

Canada, like other countries, is caught up in this power shift.
Most Canadians are aware that China is no longer "over there," a
sometimes enticing, sometimes threatening, ever-fascinating place
across an ocean. Rather it is "here," an everyday economic reality.
Canadians feel and see it when they walk the streets of their major
cities, visit a shopping mall, think about their jobs and economic
future, or take out a mortgage. Already the largest trading country
in the world and second-largest economy, China is headed to replace Canada as the largest two-way trading partner of the United
States by the end of this decade.

Canadians are only beginning to get a handle on a world order in
which America and our Western allies remain significant but are no
longer dominant. This is generating strong public reactions that co-
mingle astonishment and opportunity with uncertainty and fear.

This short book is about the evolution of Canadian China policy since 1970. It focuses on high policy issues and decisions, usually in the hands of politicians, senior officials, and diplomats in
Ottawa and missions abroad. High policy is really just one layer
of a multi-tiered relationship. The most numerous and important

actors are tens of thousands of business people, even larger numbers of Chinese students coming to Canada, hundreds of thousands of Chinese immigrants to Canada who have arrived over the past twenty years, the ghosts and descendants of missionaries past, and the legions of travellers flowing in both directions. The sinews that connect China and Canada are human interactions, commercial activities, and a myriad of institutional linkages across the Pacific.

Everyone has opinions about China while only a few are interested in the high politics, meta-narratives, and strategic dimensions of the Canada-China relationship. Most Canadians involved with China go about their business of making deals, selling, trading, investing, studying, visiting, labouring, living, and working. Trade and investment issues are by a wide margin the overriding Canadian priorities. Canadian political leaders have a thousand concerns—China being only one among them—and a major interest in constituencies and issues that get them re-elected. Rarely and only on niche issues in specific constituencies has foreign policy, much less China, arisen as a prime electoral issue. And rare is the bureaucrat who has the time or incentive to get beyond the immediate demands of managing a very complicated and difficult set of day-to-day files.

Yet high policy matters. Operationally, it sets the tone and builds the framework from which other things in a relationship flow. Intellectually, it functions as a window on perceptions, calculations, mindsets, images, and a recurring debate about Canada's role in the world and its fundamental interests and values. In terms of identity, it makes a statement about what Canada is and what role it plays in the world.

My specific focus is the high policy of engagement that has provided the frame for a constellation of interactions, the rationale for scores of initiatives, and the impetus for strong personal relations that most Canadian leaders have tried to strike with their Chinese counterparts.

As the recurrent narrative for the Canada-China story, engagement is where policy meets images, attitudes, ideology, experience, diplomacy, and calculations of commercial interest and comparative advantage. It has proven flexible and enduring, functioning variously as myth, aspiration, and strategy—as well as a target for recurring criticism. The pages that follow look at its origins and philosophic underpinnings, history and evolution, advocates and critics, current possibilities, and dilemmas. Engagement is about the mutual expectations and interactions between Canadian and Chinese leaders; it is also about an implicit covenant between Canadian policy makers and a sometimes anxious, sometimes enthusiastic Canadian public.

Engagement has underwritten Canadian policy with only temporary wobbles since 1970 and has roots that go back much farther. It has frequently been contested and occasionally eclipsed, but it has been the defining and in some ways distinctive feature of the Canadian approach to the People's Republic of China for at least half a century. Canadians came to articulate and embrace engagement well before the United States and much of the world. Ironically, Canada came close to abandoning it in the first years of the Harper Conservative government at the very moment that almost every country on earth was clambering on board its bandwagon.

The context is a moment in which the stakes of getting China policy right have never been higher and in which the premises that underlay the engagement policies of the past are being thrown into question by changes in the world as well as the shifting perceptions of policy elites and the general public at home. I ran into these shortly after the election of the first Stephen Harper minority government in January 2006 in my role as the Co-CEO of the Asia Pacific Foundation of Canada. I heard three members of the Conservative caucus, two of them in the Cabinet, describe China as "a godless totalitarian country with nuclear weapons aimed at us." The words "godless," "totalitarian," and the framing of China as an unmitigated strategic threat were jarring. They drew on images of China and a worldview far removed from the main lines of Canadian thinking for two generations. And far from being isolated to an anti-Communist fringe, they occasionally resonated with ideas across the ideological spectrum.

Getting China right is not any easier for Canadians than Americans, Australians, Koreans, or others. But it has a special dimension because the Canadian relationship with China has so often been expected to produce something more than commercial advantage and diplomatic success. Publics, and many of the policy makers themselves, have treated it as a moral enterprise. Despite the vast differences in history, culture, civilization, political and economic systems, and geography that separate Canada from China, there has been the expectation that Canada is in the business of transforming China, not just living with it. Behind the idea of helping China is the idea of changing China, "making it more normal," as an animated stranger in a Tim Hortons line once told me.

While this expectation of change may be unrealistic, hypocritical, or a touch sanctimonious, it has been recurrent and never far from the surface. The perpetual problems for our policy makers are threefold. What exactly do we expect of China and in what time frame? How do we reconcile our interest in internal Chinese affairs with other policy priorities? How do we get high-level Chinese attention and cooperation while being mindful of our primary relationship with the United States?

In a Canada where rights and freedoms are a national passion, where magnificent new museums are dedicated to human rights, dealing with an obstinate China fuels frustration and strong emotions. In a grandly ironic twist, Pierre Trudeau gave Canada both recognition of the Communist government in China and a Charter of Rights and Freedoms. Engagement has been savaged in both Canada and the United States as futile, counterproductive, unconscionable, and dangerous. Canadian values put limits on the breadth and scope of what we do with a China under Communist rule. The Chinese embrace of democracy and human rights is at best uncertain and not likely to be in our image. Different ideas about the good, the true, the beautiful, and the legitimate get in the way.

The recurring paradox of Canadian policy is that, despite all of these differences and asymmetries, all the risks and uncertainties, Canadian policy makers have tended to wager that they can occasionally influence China in ways that other countries can't. Getting Canadians ready for global China and a more sophisticated policy of engagement will be more difficult—and more essential—when they are being asked to examine core values and institutions that they once believed were built on universal principles but that now may be seen to be merely Western. The basic tenets of the post-Second World War, American-supported, liberal international order face a major challenge. The problem is particularly acute in an era of Conservative dominance in Ottawa where a philosophy of small government and anti-Communist ideology have strong resonance. Despite the dramatic shift of policy from its starting point in 2006, the current embrace of China is tactical, fragile, and conditional.

Beyond chronicling the history of engagement, my aim is to provide an intellectual rationale and some guidelines for recalibrating engagement in an era of shifting global power. Even as the main pillars of an engagement strategy are under increasing attack, it is still our best bet on how to approach a China that is increasingly important and powerful and also showing signs of becoming more assertive on the world stage. How to do it in a way consonant with both Canadian values and interests is no easy matter.

Acknowledgments

My vantage point on Canada-China relations is not as a sinologist, a diplomat, or a specialist on Canadian foreign policy. Rather, my academic work for the past thirty-five years has concentrated on trans-Pacific relations, regional security, and institution building in Asia Pacific. The stimulus for this book is the rise of China, the conflicted Canadian response, and the desire to re-establish the intellectual and policy foundations for an innovative and constructive approach to China policy.

The book is fashioned from an array of sources, including academic writings, government archives, interviews, media accounts, and personal interactions with some of the featured players. We benefited from extensive access to several hundred files that were declassified by Arthur Menzies under a special contract to the Department. More recently, the digital age has changed the character and access points to communications inside government. Particularly since the 2006 change of government, interviews have become more difficult, the control of messaging and the bureaucracy far tighter, and the government reluctant to undertake the big and open policy reviews that earlier, for better or worse, were a chronicler's treasure in taking the pulse of governmental thinking. Reliance on press accounts, conversations with cautious insiders, and best guesses about motives and decisions are the thin reeds on which the story of the Harper period is based. Discerning the China strategy and policy of the Harper government is only possible by inferring them from what the government does or doesn't do, not from a stated vision or plan.

I have been enriched by working for three decades with some of the academics, officials, and politicians most closely connected with Canadian policy and, intermittently, with some of their counterparts in Asia as part of the fertile world of track-two policy dialogues that proliferated in the 1990s. I especially benefited from two intensive programs I organized with Chinese counterparts: first, the "Canada-Chinese Seminar on Regional Multilateralism and Cooperative Security," which involved Chinese academics, research institutes, diplomats, and People's Liberation Army officers personnel between 1996 and 2000; and, more recently, the "Bilateral Dialogue on Emerging Issues in Canada-China Relations" organized in cooperation with the Shanghai Institutes of International Studies.

I owe an ongoing debt to Bernie Frolic, my partner in a decade of research and writing on Canada-China relations starting in the early 1980s. He is writing the kind of detailed, meticulously researched history of the relationship that is so badly needed, a work that has been gestating for twenty-five years. David Dewitt, Brian Job, Amitav Acharya, Pierre Lizee, David Capie, and, before his death in 2012, Tom Delworth have been close associates in working with Chinese and Asian colleagues in building policy-related dialogues since the early 1990s. We have been part of scores of meetings and an incessant trans-Pacific discussion on political and security issues in Asia, a great many of them in the past decade centred squarely on how to deal with a rising China. Jack Austin, Yuen Pau Woo, and John McArthur were supportive during my period as co-CEO at the Asia Pacific Foundation when I had a brief but upfront and personal exposure to China policy in the early years of the Harper government. And I am grateful to the Department of External Affairs, now known as the Department of Foreign Affairs, Trade and Development, for access to a large set of departmental files on China policy between 1949 and 1989 and for the opportunity to speak with or interview more than a hundred China-wallahs in the department over three decades. Bernie Frolic's forthcoming book will use these materials in far more detail than I have been able to here. In addition, I benefited from discussions about China with three former prime ministers and more than forty parliamentarians, about half of them in Cabinet.

Alvyn Austin helped in generous ways with information and interpretation about the missionary enterprise in China and its living legacies. And Suzy Dong Yikun, now an assistant professor at the Beijing Foreign Studies University, provided a great deal of assistance focused on journalistic and parliamentary coverage of Conservative-era policy making while writing her award-winning doctoral thesis.

I owe special thanks to the persistent and ever-encouraging Jennifer DiDomenico, who put the idea of such a "short" book to me two years ago, and to the three reviewers assigned by the University of Toronto Press, who constructively spotted no end of errors and ambiguities in an earlier draft.

The book has also benefited from, and been delayed by, an out-pouring of recent articles, reports, and books on key aspects of the Canada-China relationship, especially the economic dimension. In 2004, a colleague complained to me about the difficulty of finding materials for teaching about the various dimensions of the Canada-China relationship. She can now turn to a lively and wide-ranging compendium from academics and think tanks. What we still need are a full-gauged history of Canadian policy making and a systematic account of the Chinese side of the equation. What we do know about the thinking and drivers behind Chinese policy is intriguing but not yet substantial.

ENGAGING CHINA

Myth, Aspiration, and Strategy in Canadian Policy
from Trudeau to Harper

chapter one

The China Policy Problem

The hardest thing of all to accept may be a world in which the United States and its Western allies are no longer the sole, or even dominant, global power … For many Canadians this rapidly evolving world order is just plain frightening.

John Ibbitson, "What the Rise of Asia Means for Canadians,"
Globe and Mail, 24 September 2012

Until very recently China has never been a top-tier policy priority for Ottawa. Even so, China has held a central place in the international imagination of Canadians since well before they managed their own foreign policy or established an embassy in China in 1944. The epochal events of China's opening to the West, its century of upheaval and revolution, Chinese immigration to Canada (and exclusion), Canadian missionaries in China, the Pacific War, the victory of the Communists, a hot war in Korea, a Cold War that followed, a cultural revolution, an era of "Open Door" and reform, and now China's emergence as a global force have generated national attention and stirred deeply felt emotions. Since 1948 the National Film Board has made more than fifty documentaries about China. Surveys conducted for the Department of Foreign Affairs and International Trade between 2002 and 2007 showed that China was consistently viewed by Canadians as the second most important country for Canadian foreign policy after the United States, and by 2007 was ranked almost equal with the United States.

The enduring features of Canadian interactions with China lie in three domains. Commercially, the eighteenth-century export of ginseng to Asia gave way to a much larger project in building a transcontinental rail and steam line system connecting markets in Europe, North America, and Asia, the first iteration of a "Gateway" strategy that would take on new meaning in the era of global supply chains a century later. Canada was an early provider of wheat to the People's Republic of China during the desperate period in the early 1960s after the failure of the Great Leap Forward. The lure of the China market was irresistible and was joined in the 1980s by a rapid increase in Chinese exports to Canada. The volume of trade started at a low base. In 1960, the year before the first wheat sales, total two-way trade was about $13 million; the following year, after the first sales, it jumped to about $129 million. In 1970, the year that diplomatic relations were established, it was about $160 million. In 1980 it was just over $1 billion. In 1990 it exceeded $3 billion, and 1990 was also the last year in which Canada had a trade surplus with China. In 2000 it was just under $15 billion; in 2005 about $37 billion, with China posting a trade surplus of more than $22 billion; in 2012 it was just under $70 billion, with Chinese exports a little less than three times the dollar value of its imports. China is now the second-largest trading partner of Canada, the United States, and the European Union. It is Canada's second-largest export destination and likely to surpass Canada as America's largest two-way trading partner by the end of the decade. Since 2005 it has been Canada's fastest-growing trade partner, with Canada-China trade growing ten times faster than Canadian trade with the rest of the world.

Trade statistics reveal only part of the real economic value of the commercial relationship. In the past fifteen years the two economies have been increasingly closely connected through two-way investment, especially major Chinese investment in Canada since 2010, infrastructure projects, technology transfers, movements of labour and professionals, the development of trans-Pacific supply chains, and the emergence of China as a central hub in regional production systems. China has become a customer, a partner, and a competitor of major proportions. Bilateral trade statistics conceal how Canada has fared relative to other countries or as a percentage of both China's and Canada's overall trade, where the aggregate numbers are impressive but the relative weight small, especially in Canada's share of the Chinese market. China is now the largest trading partner of almost every country in Asia—Japan, South Korea, India, Taiwan, Indonesia, Thailand, and Vietnam included. It is now Africa's largest trading partner, as it is for Australia, Brazil, Chile, and New Zealand. This is not just the rise of China but, as David Shambaugh frames it, "*the spread*" of China.[1]

These statistics have been the scorecards for generations of Canadian trade officials and diplomats who have staked their careers and reputations on getting the numbers up and promoting and facilitating business in the China market. One Canadian ambassador to China in the 1980s, Richard Gorham, stated it baldly: "I don't want to change the Chinese. I want to sell Canadian goods and services to them. Our aims in China are economic, crass commercialism not geopolitical."[2] Often to the chagrin of economists, politicians have gravitated to trade statistics as benchmarks of Canadian economic performance. In 2006 and 2007 they were used in very public fashion by Conservative MPs to make the case that it was possible to confront China on human rights issues while expanding two-way trade.

Until very recently, for all the ballyhoo, China trade has had far more symbolic importance in Canada than material impact. That is changing. In the past decade, and especially since the economic crisis of 2008, China has emerged as something far more significant than a trading partner and the shop floor of the world. It is the world's largest trading nation, a global financier with foreign currency reserves in excess of $3.5 trillion in 2013, the largest foreign holder of American treasuries (valued in 2013 at $1.2 trillion), the largest net importer of oil, a major source of outward investment (now valued at about $500 billion, about $20 billion in Canada alone, and until very recently rising quickly), as well as the world's largest destination for foreign direct investment (valued in 2013 at about $2.16 trillion), and integral to regional production networks and supply chains. In 2012 China accounted for about 40 per cent of world growth.

Equally important, and in earlier years far more controversial, have been two-way movements of people. They began with the immigration of Chinese labourers to work on transportation infrastructure in Canada in the 1870s just before a smaller but no less determined group of Canadian missionaries set forth to China. Restrictions on Chinese immigration with the Exclusion Act of 1923 (repealed in 1947), the Pacific War that started in 1937, the ensuing Chinese civil war between Mao Zedong's Communist forces and Chiang Kai-shek's Nationalists, and the Communist victory severely constrained direct movement, though a large number of mainland Chinese established a connection with Canada through Hong Kong.

Interactions sky-rocketed after the Open Door of 1979, with family reunification being supplemented by large-scale migration (averaging over the last decade about 45,000 immigrants per year) from mainland China directly to Canada. There are now roughly one and a half million people of Chinese descent living in Canada. Chinese students began arriving in the early 1980s and a decade later constituted the largest source of foreign students in Canada. In 2011 there were more than 68,000 Chinese students registered at Canadian universities and schools and about 2,000 Canadian students at Chinese institutions. The number of Canadians working and living in China is far smaller but not insignificant. The Asia Pacific Foundation of Canada estimates that there are about 400,000 Canadian citizens resident in greater China, more than half of them in the Hong Kong Special Administrative Region. Tourism has flourished in both directions, as has business travel. China is now the world's largest source of tourists. In 2012 almost 300,000 Chinese citizens visited Canada and almost 325,000 Canadians travelled to China. Seventy-five non-stop flights a week now connect the two countries. The 15,000 or so young Canadians teaching English in Asia, China included, are the twenty-first-century successors to the fresh-faced missionaries of a century earlier.

The third domain has been diplomatic and strategic. To manage bilateral relations including immigration, trade, and diplomacy, the Republic of China established a mission in Canada in 1926, and Canada eventually reciprocated in 1944. As a marginal participant in Asian diplomacy—Pierre Trudeau once said that Canada had a "ringside seat on the Pacific" but did not state that we were *in* the ring—China usually loomed as a significant regional problem but one of second-tier importance. It was the domain of a small number of officials who wrestled with a series of difficult strategic questions centred on China, including the Pacific War, the Communist-Nationalist struggle, recognition of the new government of the People's Republic of China in 1949, the Korean War, U.S.-China tensions for two further decades of Cold War with China, Chinese support for insurgencies in the non-Communist world, U.S. rapprochement with China, recurring issues focused on Taiwan and Tibet, the events and aftermath of Tiananmen Square, Canada's own rapprochement with China, Hong Kong's repatriation to the mainland and the adjustment to increasing Chinese influence and capacity in its neighbourhood, multilateral institutions, and, most recently, global governance. China now has nuclear-powered submarines, an operational aircraft carrier, and a limited but sophisticated force of inter-continental ballistic missiles, plus advanced fighter aircraft, cruise missiles, and the world's second-largest fleet of drones. It puts astronauts in space, may soon do a moon landing, and can destroy satellites in orbit.

These three domains have produced a folklore about Canada-China relations and no shortage of heroes and controversies. The most important players in the Canada-China drama are the Chinese immigrants who have contributed so much to Canada. And the Canadian names associated with the relationship have legendary status: Two Gun Cohen, Norman Bethune, Jonathon Goforth, Robert McClure, Bishop William White, James Endicott, George Lesley MacKay, Chester Ronning, Alvin Hamilton, James Menzies and Arthur Menzies, Douglas Jung, Paul Lin, Pierre Trudeau, Jack Austin, David Lam, Vivienne Poy, Mark Rowswell. At least two of them—Bethune (Bai Qiuen) and Rowswell (Da Shan)—are better known in China than in their home country.

The differences in size and scale, language, culture, tradition, civilization, history, and political, social, and economic institutions are vast. China's population is greater than those of Europe and all of the Americas combined. The city of Chongqing has a population bigger than Canada's. But despite this, those who have connected Canada and China treat themselves and their impact seriously.

Personal contacts have mattered to both countries disproportionate to the number of individuals involved and in defiance of the staggering asymmetries.

The Current Policy Agenda

With the exception of Canada's relations with the United States, no other relationship is as complex, pressing, and diverse at the levels of policy and management as the one with China. Global China affects Canada in virtually every policy domain, ranging from security and diplomacy through to First Nations affairs, fisheries, and Arctic passageways. Commercially, it is important with respect to trade policy on a global, regional, and bilateral basis, including issues such as proposals for a bilateral free trade agreement, use of intellectual property, development of a next-generation Foreign Investment Promotion and Protection Agreement (FIPPA), decisions about major Chinese investments in Canada, food and product safety, air and sea transport agreements, and exports of strategic resources, including uranium. Trade policy issues stretch well beyond tariffs and quotas and include regulatory and environmental matters, the granting of market economy status to China, use of the renminbi as a reference currency, corporate social responsibility, social licensing, rule of law challenges, protection of intellectual property, and dispute resolution processes. Government heft is still needed to assist Canadian companies doing business in a hard Chinese market and, more recently, Chinese companies operating in a new Canadian one.

The agenda in international institutions includes the full set of financial, trade, and governance issues at the G20, the IMF, and the World Bank, and in regional institutions where Canada is a member, including the Asia-Pacific Economic Cooperation (APEC). In virtually every global issue of interest to Canada, China is a player, ranging from human security in Syria to climate change, control of infectious diseases, counter-terrorism, and the activities of the U.N. Security Council and regional institutions, including the Association of Southeast Asian Nations (ASEAN) Regional Forum.

On security matters the agenda stretches from the weaponization of outer space and non-proliferation through to maritime boundary disputes in eastern Asian waters, the future of the Arctic, and cyber-security.

The new dimension is China's role not just as a participant in international institutions but as a major player and, on occasion, as with the Shanghai Cooperation Organization connecting it to Central Asia and Russia, as a creator. The pattern of Chinese participation in international governance has shifted in twenty years from minimal involvement to defensive engagement to assertive action and occasional, if usually reluctant, leadership. It is uncertain whether China will emerge as a "responsible stakeholder" in a Western-led liberal order, play a more dominant role as a "rule maker" and not just a "rule taker," or try to create an alternative set of institutions, norms, and rules. But it is certain that Chinese views, interests, and priorities will be increasingly visible and influential. Canada and the West are no longer dealing with just an important country and trading partner; they are dealing with a great power with global weight.

In the second film in the Star Wars series, Luke Skywalker is framed at dusk against a sky on his home planet of Tatooine in which not one but two suns are sinking over the horizon. In September 2011, NASA scientists declared that their Kepler spacecraft had confirmed the existence of a planet, Kepler 16b, orbiting two suns. What NASA discovered is that the two suns in fact orbit each other. The current interaction between China and the United States has some interesting parallels. The U.S.-China relationship is now the most complex and important in our world and combines elements of cooperation, competition, and antagonism in a complicated and evolving blend. Several American writers, chief among them Fred Bergsten, have spoken about a "G-2 world."[3] The idea strikes many as far-fetched. China is not that strong, remains a developing society, and faces a host of huge internal problems. China may be a moon rather than a sun or even just a shooting star. Others note that a G2 is unimaginable and probably dangerous as a prescription for global order. But the "two suns" and "G2" ideas show how far perceptions have shifted in a geopolitical blink of an eye.

In this context, few doubt that Canada's livelihood and prosperity, role in global and regional institutions, and exercise of leadership in the world will increasingly depend on getting China and China policy right. What should be Canada's strategic response to the rise of China and its basic attitude and frame of mind? Should China be approached as a friend, strategic partner, ally, competitor, adversary, or enemy? Can China be encouraged to become a responsible stakeholder in the liberal international order of market capitalism, democratic institutions, and human rights that Canadians hold dear and have expended so much blood and treasure to underwrite?

Despite the Gorham assertion that Canadian aims are commercial not geopolitical, the drive for commercial gain has always coexisted with the demand for a strategic rationale that is larger than commerce and that has a moral foundation. This involves consular matters linked to the protection of Canadians abroad, extradition and deportation proceedings, and refugee claims at home. Issues of democracy, human rights, and the rule of law in China attract acute public interest in Canada. What binds together the Canadian experience with China is the credo that simply dealing with China as we deal with Mexico, France, or India is not enough; it is essential that we be instruments of change. Canadian public debates about China policy in the 1990s were chiefly concerned, in teeter-totter fashion, with whether trade or human rights should be the policy priority. Far from disappearing at a moment when China's economic leverage is in a completely different league from Canada's, in which the prospect of economic sanctions or punishment of China through trade instruments is unimaginable without horrific costs, our domestic debate still sometimes rotates around whether we should be having economic relations with a country run by a Communist government.

This came through loud and clear in the hostile media coverage of and public reactions to two decisions by the Harper government in 2012. The first was the ratification of the bilateral FIPPA that was signed with Beijing in October 2012 after eighteen years of intermittent negotiations. Both teams of negotiators were pleased with the creation of a high-standard and comprehensive agreement with new transparency provisions. A handful of experts and several politicians were not. They raised objections that go far beyond the text of the agreement to concerns about dealing with Communist interlocutors who could not be trusted. Even more negative about China was the public debate about the sale of Nexen, a Calgary-based oil and gas company, to the Chinese National Offshore Oil Corporation (CNOOC). While some of the objections focused on the precise terms of the sale and the need to maintain free-market practices, many focused on a deep distrust of China and an argument that dealing with "Chinese state-owned enterprises" was the equivalent of dealing with a state ruled by a Communist Party that was responsible for the suppression of human rights in China. The regime was characterized as stagnant, repressive, corrupt, autocratic, tyrannical, totalitarian, and set for collapse.

The Nexen and FIPPA controversies are not the end of the debate but its newest chapter. How should we navigate this immensely and increasingly complicated playing field? How can we manage a complex, high-stakes policy agenda while making a plausible case that what is in our interest can be a catalyst for significant change in a country that dwarfs Canada many times over?

The Idea of Engagement

In policy terms, the concept that has framed Canadian approaches to China since the late 1960s is something we now call "engagement." For half a century it has been the dominant narrative in telling the story of Canada-China relations, a cornerstone for diplomatic activity, and a rationale for governments pursuing a diverse set of China objectives. Every Canadian prime minister since Pierre Trudeau has used the term, even if each has given it a somewhat different shade of meaning. In defining the instruments, objectives, and timing for changing China, we have made twists and turns in focusing on China's external or domestic behaviour, the specific values that Canada is promoting, the attitude and tone of the delivery, the question of whether making China more "normal" is about China becoming more like us or just better, and whether it is necessary to oppose or work with the Communist Party and the Chinese state in order to meet Canadian objectives.

Engagement has never gone unchallenged, has sometimes been in eclipse, and has faced a chorus of sceptics and dissenting voices outside government. But it has stuck and is probably the closest thing to an abiding orthodoxy in Canada's approach to any country in Asia or the developing world. Perhaps the most perplexing aspect of Canada-China diplomacy has been the maintenance of generally successful relations with a country that Canadians have been so intent on altering, a country that knows what Canadians have been attempting while all the time deflecting, resisting, and only occasionally accommodating those efforts. It's difficult to imagine the results if Canada were to embark on a similar crusade to "engage" the United States.

What does "engagement" mean? In policy circles the term was coined during the 1960s as a way of framing a policy response to Cold War enemies—the Soviet Union, China, Cuba—in contrast to containment, isolation, and confrontation. Long before emerging as a formally articulated concept, it was an approach to dealing with the "non–like-minded."

In its narrowest formulation, "engagement" means simply having contact, establishing a relationship where one did not exist before. It signals acceptance that another state exists and needs to be addressed. There are rules of engagement for enemies and terms of engagement for friends. In its more ambitious formulations, the term refers to the aspiration to create a constructive relationship with another state with the intent to alter its behaviour and character. The aim is not simply to embrace but to change or shape. In military terms, "rules of engagement" refers to precise rules for opposing forces dealing with each other; in romantic terms, engagement is a prelude to a relationship that brings together two people with the intention of producing something that is transformative or at least demands adjustments by each partner. Views vary sharply on whether convergence and transformation are possible or realistic.

Beneath the surface of these more ambitious understandings of "engagement" are an arsenal of ideas: the idea that outliers can be socialized and learn their way into international society; the idea that under the right conditions and with the right incentives outliers can be brought peacefully into the international system; and the moral case that it is right and the pragmatic case that it is possible to bring fundamental change to the other.

In contemporary strategic thinking, engagement is seen as one of several ways to respond to a rising power that threatens to disrupt the international system. It is distinguishable from appeasement and several other policy orientations, including containment, band-wagoning, capitulation, and buck-passing. And it is generally based on rewards and incentives rather than threats or force.[4]

Almost all countries now use the term "engagement" to describe their approach to China. It has been the phrase employed by seven American presidents dating back to Richard Nixon, all of whom have stated publicly that China's prosperity and stability—its rise—are in the interests of the United States. Also of interest is the variety of adjectives that analysts and policy makers have inserted before it. A recent sampling includes the following: ad hoc, adversarial, coercive, constructive, controlled, complex, conditional, deep, dual, friendly, hidden, partial, layered, presumptive, principled, proportional and realistic, reciprocal, selective, soft, and sustainable. The term "congagement," combining "engagement" and "containment," stretches the concept to its limit.[5]

A distinctive feature of engagement Canadian style is that it predates the era of rising China and was developed to deal with the dangerous China of the Maoist period. With antecedents stretching back into the late nineteenth century, at different moments it has taken the form of an aspiration—the hope to have an impact on China; a myth—a special relationship with China built on trust that provided privileged access; a strategy—an interconnected set of actions and words intended to broaden and consolidate connections; and a wager (or faith) that even if immediate changes are not visible in Chinese behaviour they will occur over time.

Canada's engagement with China, especially in the Cold War context, was different from America's in one key respect. After 1970 and until 2006 it had continuous and widespread support among both elites and the wider public. If U.S.-China relations rode a roller coaster, Canada-China relations spun on a far less volatile merry-go-round.

The underpinning of engagement Canadian style is that the institutions and values that recent Conservative leaders have labelled freedom, democracy, human rights, and the rule of law, while imperfect and evolving, are built on universal values that are as good for China as they are for Canada. Similarly, the Westphalian notions of sovereignty and international law grew out of historical conditions that were relevant not just to Europe but on a global basis. In dealing with imperial, republican, or Communist China, most Canadians' faith in the superiority of their own fundamental values and institutions has remained firm. The issue has been how to export or inculcate those values and institutions in the most effective way. Modest means and a deferential style have not completely masked a conviction of rightness and a more-than-occasional self-righteousness.

Asian observers suggest that the missionary impulse may be stronger in Canada, if less flamboyantly trumpeted, than in the United States or other Western countries that have had an imperial presence abroad. They note the irony that a country as small as Canada, and one that is so different from China in geography, size, scale, history, civilization, and political and economic institutions, feels it can make a difference and, more importantly, feels compelled to try. It is not that Canadian thinking and policy have swung between moralism and realism; it is that moralism and realism have been inextricably interconnected in one package.

Canadians have disagreed about whether their objective is to change the very fabric of Chinese society and politics or to influence Chinese behaviour in more modest ways. But only a precious few have considered how China is changing Canada or considered that it is Canada that must now adjust to an international order not of its own making.

Is there any other country in the world to which Canadians have devoted so much attention for so long and with a more visible values-based stance? Canadians rarely talk about "engaging" the United States, India, Japan, Brazil, or Russia. Is the conflict with China the next-to-last act in the Cold War against Communism?

Would this change if China were to embrace Western-style demo-cratic institutions? Can a values-based agenda be sustained in the face of a Communist Party and state that have the capacity either to reject and resist this agenda or selectively choose to adopt only those portions of it that are consonant with their own interests and values? If there is to be a convergence, on whose terms will it take place?

At the core of our current China problem is not so much the management of issues—as far-reaching, important, and difficult as they are—but the need to reach a new consensus on an approach to China—one that can find public assent and can adequately address a radically altered international context. In the process of refurbishing and recasting engagement, it is instructive to look at its origins, social foundations, key ideas, and counter-currents over the past fifty years. Understanding high policy and getting China right depend upon addressing deeper attitudes, philosophies, pre-conceptions, and images that have not only current impact but a very long pedigree.

chapter two

Trudeau to Tiananmen

China was never a canvas on which the West could simply cast its own fever-ish imaginings—utopian or apocalyptic. But it has tried.
 ·Kevin Rudd, 2010 Morrison Lecture at the Australian National University

When the Trudeau government established diplomatic relations with the People's Republic of China (PRC) in October 1970, it opened a new chapter and book in the high politics of Canada-China relations. Trudeau's imprint was seminal. In laying out the objectives, rationale, and tone for a new approach to China and then shaping its style and diplomatic instruments, his government set in place the foundations for a thirty-five-year consensus.

It is well known that Canada was one of the first out of the "engagement" gate and that many others, including the United States, soon moved in a similar direction. Less obvious is that behind the diplomatic initiative of 1968–70 lay a century of interactions and experiences that paved the way for the Trudeau government's breakthrough and the public and elite support that coalesced around it. Others had recognized the government of the PRC earlier, including the imperial powers of Britain and France and a newly independent India, but none did it for precisely the same reasons, with the same expectations, and facing the same kind of domestic criticisms and risks.

The engagement story begins with missionaries and Cold War diplomats.

The Missionary Legacy

Students, English teachers, tourists, diplomats, and business people may be the human face of Canada in China now, but it was missionaries who were at centre stage between 1888 and 1959. They represented multiple Protestant and Catholic denominations and orders, were composed of diverse personalities and callings, and engaged in a huge spiritual undertaking to convert China to Christianity and an equally large undertaking to improve social conditions in an impoverished and conflict-ravaged land. On a per capita basis there were more Christian missionaries from Canada than from any other country. At the end of the First World War, the mainstream Protestant churches alone were supporting two universities, 270 schools, and thirty hospitals.

If bringing Christianity and seeking converts and a Christian way of life were the common goals, the mission movement, then as now, was anything but monochromatic in theology, attitudes, societal role, and political orientation. It was less an orchestrated movement than a series of loosely connected operations headed by strong individuals separated by sharp denominational and sectarian differences. Through three broad phases chronicled by Alvyn Austin as the Saving Gospel (1888–1900), the Social Gospel (1901–27), and the Political Gospel (1928–59), evangelical Protestants, liberal Protestants, and Roman Catholics (these last almost all from Quebec and mostly female) interacted with a turbulent Chinese situation and were the window on China for a large number of Canadians. They intersected with the full pageant of China's social and political revolution, the Boxer Rebellion, the collapse of the dynastic system, the birth of the Republic, the rise of the warlords, the deepening competition between the Nationalists and the Communists, the Japanese incursion into China, the civil war that followed, and the Communist victory.[1]

Assessing the missionary impact in 1907, the Methodist minister Newton Wesley Rowell stated that despite the intention of bringing 40 million Chinese to Christ, "The least result is the number of converts added to the church. The larger and more important results are the great changes wrought in the whole social [and] intellectual life [and] character of the people [of China]."[2] Looking back, an even larger impact may have been on attitudes at home in Canada through the continuous contact the missionaries maintained with sponsoring congregations by means of letters, newsletters, and visits. Lester Pearson grew up in a Methodist manse that brought him close to the missionary enterprise in China and the flow of Canadians moving in and out of China postings. Pierre Trudeau's first memory of China was making weekly donations to the St Enfance movement to save young souls in China. Canada's first three ambassadors to the People's Republic of China, and several key policy makers in Ottawa, were born in China of missionary parents. Stephen Harper, Preston Manning, and several other prominent Conservatives have been members of the Christian and Missionary Alliance Church that was active in evangelism in China throughout the missionary period. The first three heads of the School of Chinese Studies, later renamed the Department of East Asian Studies, at the University of Toronto had been missionaries at the China Inland Mission.

Linking involvement in China to a moral enterprise was hardwired in from the beginning. For seventy years Canadian missionaries strove to bring faith and God with them to the task of conversion. Despite differences in theology, temperament, and what Fred Edwards has called the "contradictions between the evangelizers who wanted to save China and the social gospellers who wanted to serve China,"[3] the common denominator was the aspiration to change China.

Political differences were often acute. Almost all of the missionaries were initially nervous about the rise of Chinese nationalism and the Japanese incursions, but they later divided on their views of Chiang Kai-shek's Guomindang and Mao's Communists. Some stuck resolutely with the Guomindang, like Canada's first ambassador to the Republic of China, Victor Odlum. The hatred for the Communists was based both on ideology and, by the late 1940s, on the painful experiences of missionaries, especially Catholic priests, at Communist hands. The stories of suffering and martyrdom were widely distributed in Catholic churches across Canada. Most, including the United Church missionaries, were scathing in their assessment of Chiang's government while being ambivalent about what the Communists could bring to the country and whether they could find an accommodation with a Communist-backed government. And some, including James Endicott, were sympathetic to the Communists' social revolution even if they disliked some of its tactics.

The missionary period ended in the early 1950s but had a long tail. Brian Evans argues that it "morphed" into Cold War anti-Communism, socialist sympathy for China's ongoing revolution, and the contemporary commitment to promote China's adoption of Western standards of human rights. The mission mentality that earlier criticized China has its echo in the call from politicians, academics, human rights groups, and journalists that "without human rights based on the individual, democracy, and the rule of law, China cannot modernize its society."[4]

The impact of missionary views and presence was amplified by the fact that, until the early 1940s, Canada had no Canadian diplomatic representation in China, so that the missionaries represented the only substantial Canadian community in the country. While a trade office had been set up in 1923, just as Ottawa was beginning to take responsibility for its own foreign affairs, there were not many commercial opportunities in a country wracked with internal upheavals. Japan seemed a better bet for commercial and political influence.

There was little room for Canadian high policy and Canada had no China strategy until the Japanese attack on Pearl Harbor made both necessary. Canada established diplomatic relations with the Republic of China and opened an embassy in Chongqing in 1944. As late as the summer of 1943 Norman Robertson was making the case in Ottawa that "a positive Canadian policy was dependent on China's ability to maintain unity and political stability."[5] Ottawa took a mainly hands-off stance during the civil war that broke out in earnest in 1946, not because of support for the Communist side but because it felt that this would be a long-term struggle with an indeterminate outcome. The Department of External Affairs (DEA) was overridden by Cabinet on some decisions, including the sale of Mosquito bombers to the Nationalists in 1946, but its new

Ambassador, T.C. Davis, looked at ways to expand commercial activities. Davis, Pearson, and Arthur Menzies, son of a missionary himself and eventually Canada's second ambassador to the PRC, did not hold rosy views of the Nationalist government and watched the civil war from the sidelines. There was little regret when the Nationalists were defeated. Plans were put in place to set up diplomatic relations with the new Communist government shortly after it took power. The realist arguments were that every effort must be made to keep China out of the Soviet orbit and that there was a prospect for working with China's new rulers. China was seen as a difficult, if distant, strategic problem with a fairly straightforward solution.

Cold War Diplomats

A series of administrative and technical delays kept Ottawa from moving parallel to the United Kingdom and India in recognizing the new government in the nine months after it was proclaimed on 1 October 1949. The week that Cabinet approved a plan for modalities, the Korean War broke out. Within five months Canada was in a direct military conflict with China. For a decade and a half after the armistice was signed in 1953, the overriding diplomatic question was when, not if, Canada would recognize the PRC. A shifting series of obstacles arose to postpone that recognition—negative public opinion, views in the United States, Chinese belligerence at key moments, the deepening American involvement in Vietnam. The preferred solution could not be implemented. The Hamlet-like story of Ottawa's tortured debate and indecision about when and how to establish diplomatic relations with the PRC is well known. The important domestic features were the political resistance to opening relations with the PRC and the continuous desire by officials and diplomats to find a way to do so.[6]

John Diefenbaker was firmly against recognition before, during, and after becoming prime minister in 1956. He and other Conservatives, chief among them Elmer Mackay, as well as several Social Credit politicians, repeatedly made the case against recognition and Communist China's entry into the United Nations. They argued that recognition was not just a matter of diplomatic convenience but would be a sign of moral approval and should not be considered until China changed its international behaviour. In November 1957 Diefenbaker stated in the House of Commons that his government would not recognize the Communist government of China until it "expiates its wrong doing under international law … Recognition would be interpreted as recognition of Communism as such."[7] The case for the wheat sales in 1960 and 1961 was made on strictly commercial and domestic political grounds, and was not viewed as opening a bridge to China or an attempt to affect its domestic or international policies. Alvin Hamilton, the major architect of the sales, became an active apostle of a more constructive and multi-dimensional relationship with China and made the alluring case about a single market of 700 million people under single management. Diefenbaker consistently emphasized the importance of preserving links to Taiwan.

The amount of attention China received in the House of Commons between 1949 and 1982 was considerable, second only to discussion of the United States. Parliamentary views on China policy during the Cold War broke mainly along party lines. Howard Green and Donald Fleming took positions similar to Diefenbaker's and later received quiet Liberal support from C.D. Howe and James Gardiner. China was described by Social Credit members as "expansionist," "bloodthirsty," "Soviet dominated," and "an insatiable monster." John Blackmore from southern Alberta, the first leader of what became the Social Credit Party of Canada, spoke of "the Yellow Peril under Red lacquer" and pronounced unalterable opposition to recognition and U.N. admission that would condone enslavement."[8]

The view inside DEA was rather different. Internal reviews of China policy during the Diefenbaker government conducted by Sidney Smith in 1958, and then again in 1963 during the first minority government of Lester Pearson, all offered a consistent strategic rationale that challenged the wisdom of isolating China and instead recognized what were the facts on the ground. Many inside the department called for a "peaceful engagement" of China, though few were optimistic in the 1950s that recognition or admission to U.N.

membership would happen soon.[9] In 1963, the newly appointed secretary of state for external affairs, Paul Martin, called for a "progressive attitude" and "broadening contacts at a variety of levels in an endeavour to penetrate the curtain of ignorance and the blunt the edge of ideological differences."[10]

Paul Martin's views were important in another way as well. The issue of seating the PRC in the United Nations had been connected with the recognition issue from the outset and was characterized by endless diplomatic manoeuvres in U.N. circles. Martin did not sympathize with Chinese Communism but instead was deeply committed to strengthening the United Nations system, including its specialized agencies, through universal participation. He did not believe that the United Nations could meet its full potential without PRC membership and called in August 1963 for "a realistic and yet progressive attitude."[11]

Lester Pearson embodied the ambivalence of the era. His analysis of events in China before the Communists came to power was far closer to that of T.C. Davis than of Victor Odlum. As a diplomat, foreign minister, and prime minister he spoke of the "cruelties and tyrannies" of the government in Beijing but repeatedly used the argument that Communist China was a reality and that its isolation encouraged recurring crises. He encouraged various trial balloons, starting immediately after the Korean armistice. But after every review he came to the conclusion that the timing was not right. "Surely peace with Washington is more important than praise in Peking," he wrote to Paul Martin in June 1966. Two years later, in the United Church Observer, he defended his decision not to act: "When you have a division of public opinion inside your own country and there is no great impelling urgency, morally or politically, to take action, then your relations with your neighbour, with the United States, become important in respect to that issue." In the words of John English, "the China question had moved from the periphery but not to the centre" of Pearson's priorities.[12]

Diplomats, including Pearson, had for twenty years been making the case that contact with Communist China was necessary, and that a positive approach to mainland China and its inclusion in the world community would be productive. Containment and isolation were seen as a dead end.

Around them, the climate of opinion, still divided, was shifting. On the recognition issue, national opinion polls indicated that in 1950 before the Chinese intervention in the Korean War 38 per cent supported recognition and 39 per cent opposed it. In 1959, 32 per cent supported and 44 per cent opposed. In 1964, 51 per cent were in support and 34 per cent opposed; in 1969, 52 per cent were in support and 28 per cent opposed.[13] A Liberal Party conference in October 1966 passed a resolution in support of recognition and U.N. admission.

A change of policy was coming, too. A month after Pearson's morally conflicted interview in the *Observer*, Pierre Trudeau, the new leader of the Liberal Party of Canada, announced on 29 May 1968 that he would move to recognize the PRC and see it seated in the United Nations while taking account of the existence of a separate government in Taiwan.

Trudeau's China

The rationale that Trudeau gave for his 1968 opening to China did not come as a surprise. His two trips to China, in 1949 and 1960, provided an extraordinary glimpse into China in civil war and Maoist mobilization. No Canadian leader before or since has had such grounded intensity of experience with China before entering political life. In his 1949 trip he criticized Western countries for the political error of "refusing to recognize the existence of those who rule a quarter—soon to be a third—of the human race" and the economic error of hesitating "to increase trading relations with the most formidable reservoir of consumption and production that has ever existed." He also took aim at the "spiritual error" of the West in "perpetuating the established identification between Christianity and the most reactionary interest of the West, notably in linking the future of a certain kind of missionary effort to the return to power of Chiang Kai-shek."[14]

As prime minister, Trudeau offered a precise and consistent rationale that was almost exclusively geopolitical. Though convinced that a major reorientation was needed in foreign policy and that DEA needed shaking up, before negotiations began, he echoed in a May 1968 comment the department's arguments of the past twenty years. China must become a member of the world community, he argued, because many of the major world issues "will not be resolved completely or in any lasting way unless and until an accommodation has been reached with the Chinese nation," adding that "I would be in favour of any measures, including recognition on suitable terms, that can intensify the contacts between our two countries and thus normalize our relations and contribute to international order and stability."[15] China was too big and too important to be isolated from the rest of the world. Critical questions of peace, war, disarmament, and nuclear weaponry could not be settled without its participation in the community of nations. In his "colossus and conundrum" speech in May 1968 he addressed the need to know China better and reduce its unpredictability. "Canada has long advocated a positive approach to Mainland China and its inclusion in the world community. We have an economic interest in trade with China ... and a political interest in preventing tension between China and its neighbours, but especially between China and the United States."[16]

In 1970 his government's *A Foreign Policy for Canadians* stated that the negotiations underway with the Chinese were undertaken in "the hope that Canada would be able to make a contribution towards bringing China into a more constructive relationship with the world community."[17]

The case for recognition was *realpolitik* and tied to China's foreign behaviour. There was no hint that a diplomatic opening would change China's domestic institutions or society. When asked in 1987 about why he had felt so strongly about moving on the China issue in 1968, he spoke of a Cartesian desire for "consistency" in dealing with China, among several other issues, and "solving an immediate problem that needed to be solved."[18]

Other emotions, images, and judgments surfaced in later statements. Returning from his first official visit to China in October 1973, Trudeau spoke in the House of Commons about the sympathy of China's leaders for Canada's diplomatic objectives and of his own empathy for China's revolution and some of the accomplishments of its Communist leaders. "It has not been the vastness of

the Pacific that has acted as a barrier between Canada and China,"
he argued. "The gulf has been found all too often in the minds of
those of us who are unwilling to recognize the magnitude of one
of the most significant revolutions in the history of the world and
the extension of basic human amenities to hundreds of millions of
persons to whom they had been denied for millennia."[19]

Later, looking back on the issue, he and his co-author, Ivan
Head, his principal foreign policy adviser of the time, wrote about
the Chinese as "a dignified, accomplished race. To fail to recognize
the undoubted successes of the communist regime would be fool-
hardy." They added something more:

A China open to the world would be subject to the same diplomatic persuasion as other countries, and could be expected over time to adjust its
political, economic, and social practices to *bring them into harmony with
international norms*. Of equal importance, this ancient civilization was
given the opportunity to share its accomplishments with others, and to
reap the recognition it deserved for uniting a disparate population and
setting in motion policies to deliver health care and education to hundreds of millions of persons who had never been exposed to either since
the Sun Yat-sen revolution of 1911.

For all China's seeming fragility, however, the two of us shared in
common the unshakeable belief that [China] would in future become
one of the two or three most influential countries in the world. For that
reason it must not be allowed to assume that it was without friends, or
without responsibility to the international community at large. Canada's
influence, as always, was limited, but it should continue to be exerted
with that future in mind.[20]

The central lines of Trudeau's views on China were not substantially different from those of mainstream liberal internationalists
in Canada and in the United States. American China specialists,
including John Fairbank and Robert Scalapino, also understood
the forces propelling the Chinese revolution, the kind of legitimacy
it bestowed on its Communist leaders, and the need for bringing
China into the international community. They held in common the
idea that over time China might indeed work in harmony with

what we now call Western norms, though it would not adopt them completely. What made Trudeau distinctive was that he departed radically from the wisdom of the Catholic church in Quebec, which adamantly opposed opening relations with China. He seemed more influenced by Jesuit teachers attuned to social context than the natural law universalisms of mainstream Catholic orders and evangelical Protestant denominations.

Conservative critics pounced in the 1960s, accusing him of being soft on socialism and Communism and holding leftist sympathies for Cuba, China, and the Soviet Union. A later generation of neoconservatives denounced his cultural relativism for appreciating neither the level of misery in China (his 1960 visit coincided with the famine that followed the disastrous Great Leap Forward) nor the tyranny of Mao's rule (he moved ahead with negotiations at precisely the moment the Cultural Revolution was at full boil). The cultural relativism charge was that he did not hold China to the same standards as his own country and accepted cultural differences. One critic who deplored the opening to China charged that Trudeau was not only naive but "harboured a deeply illiberal admiration for Mao's China." In so doing he betrayed the cause of liberal internationalism defined as "the advance of universally recognized and widely accepted human rights and the creation of effective and legitimate international institutions."[21]

Even relatively empathetic observers of Trudeau felt some unease. His principal biographer, John English, identifies Trudeau's "overly sanguine view of China," his "naïveté" about regimes on the left, and his admiration for some of China's Communist leaders, Zhou Enlai in particular. English explains this on the basis of Trudeau's anti-establishment attitude against stern anti-Communism, a desire to break down the differences between East and West in the nuclear age, and private anxieties about China that he rarely expressed in public.[22]

The paradox is that the person who led to an opening with Communist China and who cemented high-level personal relations with its leaders was also the person deeply committed to advancing rights and freedoms in Canada. Trudeau's own view of this was that the two countries needed to be looked at in their time as well as in their historical and civilizational context. He seemed agnostic on whether it was reasonable to expect or predict that over time a China inside the world community would resemble Western societies and embrace their values and institutions. His universalisms, if he held them, were complicated; he saw the differences between societies in shades of grey, not black and white; and his sense of history was fluid.

The architects of recognition, including Trudeau, never made the case that fundamental change within China would be automatic. At the same time, none of them believed that any kind of political or social change would occur without an end to China's diplomatic isolation. The implicit reasoning of the Liberal foreign-policy elite of the late 1960s was that it was unrealistic even to begin to think about substantial change in Mao's China, that there would be something gained by ending China's isolation, and that there was little that Canada or any other country could do to shape China's future through direct intervention. If fundamental change was unrealistic, occasional influence was at least imaginable.

It has recently come to light that Chinese officials were paying very close attention to Trudeau's views, though from an angle few if any in Canada then understood. In November 2010 two former Chinese diplomats, one of them Mei Ping, the longest-serving Chinese ambassador in Canada, presented the results of their examination of the documentary record in the Chinese Ministry of Foreign Affairs related to the recognition negotiations. The negotiations were taking place at the height of the Cultural Revolution and were carefully managed by Zhou Enlai, who was in the midst of complex negotiations of his own with Mao and the four other members of the Standing Committee of the Politburo. The Chinese leadership and officials in the Ministry of Foreign Affairs knew a great deal about Trudeau and followed his comments on China carefully. The leadership was facing the choice of which country would offer the best prospect for setting the stage for a new chapter in opening China's international relations. Though both Italy and Belgium were signalling interest, Beijing chose Canada. Canada was selected on the grounds that it was close to the United States, "somewhat independent" of the United States, and interested in more than commercial relations. This third calculation was built on the view that Trudeau had a view of world order and the Cold War that made him a likely supporter of working with China on issues like U.N. admission. Unbeknownst to either side, there was a coincidence of strategic interests in having Canada play a middle power role in bringing China in from the cold.[23]

The Chinese reading was perceptive, and Canadian officials proceeded to support mainland China's admission into the United Nations. The Canadian recognition initiative established a formula for dealing with the status of Taiwan and was in the first wave of a series of negotiations pursued by other countries. Opposition to the PRC's entrance to the United Nations dissolved, and the PRC occupied the China seat in 1971.

Constructing a Relationship

With recognition, China shifted from being an exotic sideshow, an intractable Cold War problem, and a market for Canadian wheat, to a significant diplomatic enterprise. In the midst of the FLQ crisis, the announcement of 13 October 1970 was front-page news though not the top headline. The debate and rancour in the House of Commons faded away, presaging a political consensus—though not a unanimous one—that would hold for thirty-six years. Within a decade thousands of Canadians began deepening linkages in fields ranging from business and education to friendship associations and twinning. What had been seen by some as a risky initiative when launched in 1968 turned into a major domestic and international success. It proved popular at home and helped put in train a series of diplomatic moves, including the rapprochement in U.S.-China relations and an avalanche of recognitions of the PRC using the Canadian formula on the status of Taiwan. Then Secretary of State for External Affairs Mitchell Sharp later claimed that the recognition of China and the quick expansion of relations with the PRC was the most important foreign policy achievement of his time in government.

In the halcyon days of new beginnings, Trudeau set the tone, and a group of motivated officials, headed by DEA, turned to building a relationship from the ground up, first cementing basic arrangements for commercial, diplomatic, and political interaction. Commercially, the government ramped up efforts to help Canadian businesses understand and penetrate the China market. Diplomatically, the machinery of representation was set up in both capitals. Canada curtailed diplomatic relations with Taiwan and proceeded cautiously with establishing alternative representative arrangements until the mid-1980s. Canadian diplomats were extremely sensitive to Chinese positions on Taiwan and Tibet, including through the difficult period of securing Chinese, and restricting Taiwanese, participation in the Montreal Olympics in 1976. A variety of unresolved issues from the pre-Communist period were quietly settled. Internationally, Canada facilitated China's entry into the United Nations and its specialized agencies and later pushed for its inclusion in the World Bank and the International Monetary Fund (IMF).

Trudeau's 1973 visit provided an opportunity for smiles and celebration, described in the briefing books prepared by DEA as the "logical highpoint in the very considerable number of personal exchanges that have characterized relations between the two countries in the past three years." The aim was "to enhance the broadly sympathetic atmosphere that has developed and to give a more permanent character to Canada's present advantageous position ... that will carry over into the 'post-honeymoon' period." Relations were described as "warm and friendly," "active but not intensive," and "more extensive and superficial than intensive and substantial." A "fund of goodwill" was fuelled by an emotional attachment to Bethune and Trudeau and a strategic calculation that Canada was a "well-meaning and sincere power with [a] generally benign influence in the Western alliance."[24]

The briefing books also struck a note of realism about the source and durability of the special position Canada seemed to hold. To the extent that Canada ever had a privileged status, it was not predominantly determined by any factor intrinsic to Canada but almost exclusively by the fact that Canada was the first Western country of any significance to recognize China after 1964. DEA worried about romanticized views of China in Canada that had accompanied the mild euphoria of the early recognition period. The Cultural Revolution could be rekindled at any moment. Other competitors, including Australia, Japan, European countries, and the United States were following in the Canadian path and there was concern that the Chinese would "close out the emotional debt." An instrumental concern about keeping that emotional bond alive would occupy Canadian officials for most of the next forty years.

A simple trade agreement signed during Trudeau's visit consolidated Canada's position as the first supplier of wheat, potash, and plant technology. Perhaps most significantly it included a family reunification agreement that would see the first immigration from China to Canada in a generation.

The reclamation of Norman Bethune was a first step. Bethune was a Canadian Communist known for his innovation of mobile blood transfusion services during the Spanish civil war and then for his efforts as a field surgeon supporting the Communist forces during their conflict with the Japanese and the Guomindang. He died in Yenan in 1939 and was immortalized in an essay published by Mao Zedong about his absolute selflessness, an essay still read by school children in many parts of China. The Trudeau government purchased his birthplace in Gravenhurst, Ontario, in 1973 and converted it into a museum. For Canadian governments, Liberal and Conservative, Bethune was an object of opportunity, a useful door opener in China, even if seen as dubious at home. Whether Chinese officials actually knew or cared about the "selfless internationalist" of the period of anti-Japanese resistance was difficult to measure, but they knew his name and knew he was Canadian. Mutual fascination with and crass manipulation of the Bethune brand would be recurring hallmarks of a relationship short on heroes known in both countries.

The visit struck an emotional note and enlarged the myth of a special relationship that would hover in Canada-China relations for a generation. Throughout the Trudeau years, during the Progressive Conservative interregnum of Joe Clark's government in 1979 and then after Brian Mulroney's sweep to power in 1984, the direction was fixed: establish personal relations at the highest levels possible, respect China's red-line concerns about its sovereignty, and put in place as many layers of connections as possible.

The bilateral aid program that Canada unveiled in 1981 was to play a critical role as funder and catalyst in a state-led relationship. Canada's first with a Communist country, the program had been under consideration since Zhou Enlai mentioned to Trudeau during the 1973 visit that the trade balance was heavily weighted in Canada's favour. In 1980, Bo Yibo, a visiting Chinese vice-premier, signalled that China would be receptive to a Canadian program. In announcing the program in February 1981, the secretary of state for external affairs, Mark MacGuigan, framed it "as a way of continuing the process of drawing China into the world community." Later, in 1984, an internal review by the Canadian International Development Agency (CIDA) highlighted that Canadian objectives were to help "strengthen the tendency within China toward more open, tolerant policies and to cultivate China as a partner in development, commerce and international geo-politics." Canadian business leaders had more pragmatic goals of gaining help for their efforts to penetrate what many felt was a "spoiled market" that could not be approached on a strictly commercial basis.[25]

Marcel Masse, the president of CIDA, captured the zeitgeist of both his agency and the moment when he stated in 1980 that Canada's aim in China should be "the multiplication of contacts at the thinking level." A student and scholar exchange had been established soon after recognition, as had a program for seconding a Canadian academic to serve as "sinologist in residence" in the Canadian Embassy in Beijing. What Masse had in mind was something on a much larger scale. CIDA funding fuelled significant projects for cooperation and capacity building that met Chinese needs for overseas training and the acquisition of management and technological skills. These were urgent priorities for China as Deng Xiaoping's Open Door policies of economic reform took hold in 1979. Canadian universities and community colleges were key players. Towns, cities, and provinces enthusiastically created twinning relationships with Chinese counterparts. Sports teams, cultural groups, and musical groups moved in both directions, often with federal government support.

There were detractors. John Diefenbaker continued to raise concerns about the abandonment of Taiwan. Occasional speakers in the House, especially Otto Jelinek, raised concerns about too deep an embrace of Communist China. Michel Gauvin, the Canadian ambassador in Beijing from 1980 to 1982 and the first ambassador not born in China to Canadian missionaries, steadfastly opposed Ottawa's plans for opening an aid program with a Communist country. He made the case that Deng and his associates "are old and cannot offer any real guarantee that the present limited liberal tendency will bear the fruits hoped for." It was impossible to justify an aid program in light of "the non-existence of human rights in China," the sentencing of Wei Jingsheng to fifteen years in prison, and the fact that China gave priority to the development of nuclear weapons over economic development and people's living standards.[26]

"Special relationship" or not, the construction of a comprehensive relationship with China had high-level political support, general public approval, hinted that Canada continued to punch above its weight in diplomatic interactions with China, and was receiving certain commercial advantages as trade gradually expanded. In January1984, six months before he stepped down as prime minister, Pierre Trudeau was hosting Premier Zhao Ziyang's speech to Parliament in Ottawa. As the *Globe and Mail* correspondent in China wrote, Canadian officials in Beijing "are hard pressed to find a single bone of contention lodged in the craw of Sino-Canadian relations." The absence of major crises, outstanding historical claims, and entangling alliances of the sort that complicated relations with the Soviet Union made the relationship relatively smooth sailing.

Mulroney

Despite speculation that a newly elected majority Progressive Conservative government would take a fresh look at China, including relations with Taiwan, Mulroney's approach to China unfolded as a seamless continuation of previous policy. After hinting that human rights would be a major feature of Canadian policy in contexts wider than South Africa, he told Parliament on 11 October 1985 that

"I have indicated to the House, to the premier of China and the President of China the fact that the intention of this Government is to pursue the policy set out by my predecessor, Mr. Trudeau, with which I agree. We have honoured that in all circumstances."

Progressive Conservative attention focused on expanding trade globally, and in Asia in particular. To Mulroney's caucus, keen on economic renewal, China was a country of increasing economic and strategic importance for Canada and the world. A Special Joint Committee of the House of Commons and Senate pointed to a "slight advantage" that Canada had in China because of its early recognition. Two-way trade rose to $2 billion in 1985, and there were signs of economic and social opening.[27] Earlier, in a March 1985 Government Green Paper, *Competitiveness and Security,* China had been described as a rising force in the international marketplace, of growing strategic importance for Canada, and "a nuclear weapons state with superpower potential reopening its contacts with the West."

Mulroney hosted President Li Xiannian and Vice-president Li Peng in July 1985. During the visit President Li described Canada as "a trustworthy partner in economic and geopolitical terms" with "a record of generosity and cooperation in using its comparative wealth." The DEA briefing book noted that a "remarkable degree of confidence has been established ... given the limits that history, geography and differing political viewpoints impose." Ten months later Mulroney made his first official trip to China (he had been there only once before on a business mission in 1979) where he met with Deng Xiaoping, President Li, Premier Zhao Ziyang, and Communist Party General Secretary Hu Yaobang. During the visit Canada agreed to give China a $2 billion line of credit, double the size of the aid program, and sign a double taxation agreement. Mulroney was impressed with Deng's view that Gorbachev had made a great mistake in initiating political reforms before economic ones. On the flight returning home he wrote in his diary, "Much remains to be done in expanding the relationship but persistent work by successive Canadian prime ministers, principally Pierre Trudeau, is clearly paying off. I think the extent and quality of my meetings with Chairman Deng, the premier, the president and the general secretary clearly indicate the value of this highly advantageous relationship."[28] Later that year the two countries set up an annual bilateral political consultation among senior officials.

Not everyone thought the commercial side of engagement was paying off. Canada's ambassador in Beijing, Richard Gorham, wrote to headquarters on 7 February 1987 that, despite fifteen years of efforts, "the overall return on our investment (over and above Chinese expressions and sentiments of friendship and goodwill) has not/not been impressive." He added that there is "no evidence that the lustre of the maple leaf or the memory of Norman Bethune ... have persuaded Chinese negotiators to opt for sourcing their requirements in Canada unless the price is right." He went on to make the case for a smarter use of Canada's limited resources, opining that Australia was getting a lucrative part of the wheat market share without matching Canada's $100 million in bilateral aid.

The human rights element of engagement was on the Mulroney government's agenda, though not as a top priority. In 1985, Canadian officials were instructed not to raise human rights issues directly with their Chinese counterparts but rather to cooperate with organizations like Amnesty International in pursuing the cases of individual dissidents and prisoners of conscience in China. That year, eight applicants for refugee status in Canada were accepted and twenty-one were refused. The briefing book prepared for Mulroney's 1986 visit advised that, because of the absence of high-profile dissidents in China, China's refusal to discuss internal matters, and the positive feelings in the West about China, it was best for Mulroney to indicate informally to Chinese officials that Canadian citizens were concerned about the matter. "High profile treatment of this sensitive issue could likely mar the atmosphere of your visit and is unlikely to generate a satisfactory Chinese response." Instead, it was seen as more rewarding to "continue to engage the Chinese into a growing web of exchanges (Interpol, etc.) which would draw China into the 'human rights mainstream' " and arrange an exchange of ministers of justice. "Although China's record on human and civil rights is a relatively poor one," it concluded, "Canadians generally seem prepared to overlook this area of concern. Exceptions include Catholic Church groups and Amnesty International."

The political situation in China was perceived to be improving slightly. As noted in the briefing book, "China is definitely not in the process of becoming a Western-style liberal market economy and while China's reforms will likely be marked by various shifts and reassessments in the years ahead, there is greater hope today than at any time in the PRC's history that a pragmatic and more open-minded approach to China development and relations with the outside world will prevail."

After the trip, Prime Minister Mulroney tasked Secretary of State for External Affairs Joe Clark to initiate a major review of China policy with the intention of creating an "effective, dynamic, coordinated course for bilateral relations with China" and better coordination of governmental and private-sector efforts. The eventual report to Cabinet and the preceding exchanges between DEA headquarters and the Canadian embassy in Beijing give a revealing glimpse into official thinking of the time. An internal assessment in February argued that China was of growing importance because of its cultural achievements, geopolitical strength, and significance as a market. Public support was judged to be intense and capable of supporting a deeper relationship, especially if it generated jobs. The embassy in Beijing responded that "Canada appears mesmerized with China but we should discourage this in favour of a more realistic attitude … Dialogue will not produce Chinese recognition of Canada as a world mover and shaker." It maintained that China was a Marxist-Leninist state "with more in common with the USSR and Eastern Europe than its Asian neighbours. China's relations with the outside world are characterized by much of the same selfishness and self-centredness to be found in Soviet and East European relations with the outside, amplified by historical Middle Kingdom attitudes of sublime superiority." The message noted concerns about Chinese espionage in Canada, a likely slowing of Chinese growth that year, the difficulties Canadian companies were having in making a profit in China, and the fact that for the first time China would soon have a trade surplus with Canada.[29]

On 31 March 1987, the Cabinet Committee on Foreign and Defence Policy approved "A Canadian Strategy for China" that aimed to

"capitalize on Canada's fascination with China to seize opportunities and position ourselves for 2000 when China will be a major world power with a GNP of $1 trillion." It outlined nineteen
steps, boiled down from twenty-six in the initial DEA report, built
on the foundation of essential programs and agreements already
in place.[30] The period of "fascination" and "romanticized interest"
was over and needed to be replaced with a period of "real potential benefits for Canada" via a better understanding of China, better
management practices in government, and improved consultative
and cooperative mechanisms. It recommended building an aid program that was about development, not politics. Significantly, human rights were not mentioned in the memo or the accompanying
work plan.

If the aim of engaging China was to influence China, the focus
was very heavily on moderating Chinese external behaviour and
supporting the forces of economic reform that would have direct
benefit to Canada. The American-led policy of isolation and containment had long since melted away. China's foreign policy in the
political, security, and above all economic domains was substantially different in 1985 than it had been in 1970 when China was in
the midst of the Cultural Revolution. Few expected or demanded
substantial political reform, though many inferred that the seeds
of reform were being sown.

In early 1989, Mulroney delivered passionate speeches on human
rights and universal values, underpinning his approach to South Africa
and Eastern Europe. The omission of China had been striking. The call
for "moral leadership" by both Mulroney and Clark seemed hollow
to some in caucus and Cabinet. Barbara McDougall, a Progressive
Conservative MP from Ontario, had already announced that she would
never visit China until it stopped abusing human rights. For a West that
was watching Communist systems crumble in Europe, expectations
were high that the democratic winds would blow in China.

Then came June 4.

After seven weeks of intensive media coverage, the events in and
around Tiananmen Square shook China, the world, and the bud-
ding bilateral relationship. On 15 May, in a whopping understate-
ment, the embassy sent a message to Ottawa that, "If it takes place,

repression will attract considerable attention abroad. Scores of journalists in town will be exposed to current events and sensitized to them as never before."

Tiananmen posed a profound challenge and shifted the terms of discussion about China and China policy and who was participating in it. In the course of a few short weeks, as Bernie Frolic notes, "Views of China changed substantially, from a vague sense of exoticism before the massacre, to a view of a harsh authoritarian regime led by aging leaders who killed their own citizens."[31]

With the shock, anger, and sense of betrayal that followed, the chemistry of the relationship turned almost overnight. Comprehensive engagement had been supported on the grounds that it laid the seeds for economic reform and that liberalizing tendencies, albeit weak and fragmentary, were following in its wake. Would engagement survive?

chapter three

Strategic Partnership

Our policy towards China has been based on engagement. The ability to sit and talk about all and any issues, human rights, environment, trade and investment, global security. We were able to hold a high level of engagement because we took a longer view of where China was going and where we could act as an interlocutor. And China on its own accord has developed a freer and more progressive society than it has probably ever been.

Senator Jack Austin, speech at the University of British Columbia,
4 October 2007

Engagement policy is based on the great myth that we in the West can change China. It holds that if we are nice enough, China will slowly but surely evolve into a market economy, a pluralist society and, voila, one day it is a moderate middle democracy. It may take a while for people to realize it, but engagement with China is failing.

Ross Munro, quoted in Miro Cernetig, "Dragons and Doves,"
Globe and Mail, 16 January 1999

Engagement had been popular and well understood, and conformed to broader public views about Canada's role in the world. All three of its foundations were shaken, as was China, by the events in Tiananmen Square. Unlike protests in Cairo's Tahrir Square a generation later, the demonstrations did not bring down a regime. But human rights took new prominence in the Canadian equation, not just around the individual cases of activists and dissidents but as focused on the broader social contract between the Chinese people and the Chinese Communist Party.

Some portrayed this as the end of innocence or naivety about the nature of Chinese Communist rule. For the architects of the Canada-China relationship the events of June 1989 were shocking but not transformational. They dashed expectations that political reform would move in lock step with economic reform. Intellectual recalculation combined with fevered public sentiments to produce a sober reassessment of premises and possibilities, but not a major or long-term reorientation of policy.

Expressing his horror and outrage at a "tragedy of global proportions," Joe Clark, as foreign minister, stated during an emergency debate in the House of Commons on 5 June that "We had hoped and believed that China was on the road to extensive and fundamental reform ... Many among us believed that China would somehow manage the pressure for such change by becoming more democratic, more open and more respectful of its own people." The carnage in the streets undermined the "positive signs of a nation in the process of change."[1]

The Mulroney government expressed its revulsion with the level of brutality and condemned the Chinese government's action in the strongest terms. It undertook the evacuation of Canadian citizens and coordinated assistance to Canadians living in China. On 30 June Clark outlined that Ottawa had temporarily recalled its ambassador, implemented targeted sanctions against military sales, reviewed Canada's $2 billion line of credit for China, reviewed celebratory events on a case-by-case basis, deferred high-level exchanges (no bilateral visits, though face-to-face meetings did occur on the margins of multilateral gatherings), suspended CIDA support for and involvement with some large-scale development projects, and delayed approval of several new CIDA projects already negotiated. Other measures included suspension of nuclear cooperation consultations, the modest program of defence cooperation, and the exchange of military exports. Radio Canada International began broadcasting into China in Mandarin on 20 June. In the ensuing months the embassy established a new staff position focusing exclusively on human rights.

Ottawa extended the visas of Chinese students and scholars resident in Canada. Almost all of the students, numbering about 10,000, eventually qualified for permanent residence status. The government also accelerated immigration procedures for members of the students' families. Provinces and cities suspended their twinning relationships. A York University group demanded to "send the pandas back," unaware that the pandas had never been delivered.

Prime Minister Mulroney told a Vancouver audience in June that "It's a calamity for them and it's a calamity for the breath of fresh air that was a democratic impulse running through China."[2] At the G7 meeting later that summer he pushed other leaders to suspend arms sales and World Bank loans and to halt high-level political contacts. A year later he opposed Japanese efforts to lift the sanctions. In May 1991 his trade mission to Japan and Hong Kong intentionally bypassed Beijing.

While these measures sent signals, they did not derail the engagement train. Ottawa did not cut diplomatic relations or trade, impose general sanctions, or terminate the aid program as members of the opposition and angry citizens' groups demanded. Only three months after Tiananmen Square, DEA approved an Export Development Corporation loan to China on the basis of classic engagement theory. "We have seen elsewhere in the socialist world that the modernization of these societies can serve to advance political change," Joe Clark stated to the *Toronto Star*, on 5 August 1989. There is "no gain to the cause of reform in China to be had from a policy which is 'anti-China.' A poorer and more isolated China is not in the broad interest of the Chinese people."[3] John Turner, leader of the Liberal opposition, denounced the decision as "moral turpitude," another example of a politician taking a moral stance on human rights in opposition as compared to more nuanced formulations when in power.

Clark's statement in the House in the immediate aftermath of Tiananmen had already made the rationale clear: "We value the friendship between our two peoples. We have not become, and will not become anti-China ... We must try to avoid measures that would push China towards isolation."[4] Even during the period when high-level contacts were deferred, Joe Clark met his Chinese counterpart during an international conference in Cambodia in September 1989.

In August 1990 Bernie Frolic characterized the government's response as "a moderate rebuke rather than an angry outcry" and later added that "China is big and important and we may have less influence than we thought. We may not be able to impose our values even if we are convinced we are right."[5] Former ambassador Richard Gorham observed in a private interview that only the starry-eyed had been affected by Tiananmen. It revealed nothing new about the regime and didn't produce a major shift in government calculations. China remained "a sacred cow that eats Canadian wheat."[6]

When the Dalai Lama visited in September 1990, Prime Minister Mulroney declined to see him or invite him to address Parliament. By 1991 academics and business leaders were calling for the restoration of high-level visits. Later in 1991 the minister of agriculture visited China, followed in 1992 by the minister of international trade as part of a step-by-step resuscitation of high-level contacts. Even Barbara McDougall, appointed Clark's successor as foreign minister in May 1991, took a measured position. Earlier she had vigorously attempted to push a stronger human rights agenda, but in office she restored and expanded mechanisms for two-way consultation and exchange, including bilateral visits. Canada made special efforts to involve China in regional security discussions focused on building multilateral institutions and managing maritime issues, including the South China Sea. The Department of National Defence began direct exchanges with the People's Liberation Army. Canadian ambassadors were speaking about human rights at the Central Party School on the rule of law and democracy, the Canadian Bar Association was working with the All China Lawyers Association, and diplomats were pushing to get information into the Chinese media about human rights.

At a private dinner that Mulroney hosted at 24 Sussex Drive in May 1993, not long before he left office, for Vice-premier (and later Premier) Zhu Rongji, Mulroney signalled, as he later recalled, that Canada "would be prepared to fully engage with China in the years ahead," though it would do so cautiously because of human rights concerns.[7]

Public disquiet about China began to consolidate around three themes—human rights, democratic development, and good governance. In the period prior to Tiananmen all three had been an element of policy thinking in Ottawa, though not as urgent, widely publicized, or top-drawer priorities. For more than a decade after Tiananmen, the public, parliamentary, and media discourse about China policy focused on the tension between a robust commercial agenda and the promotion of Canadian values. The "trade versus human rights" debate took a tenacious hold on public attention. Even as policy remained consistent, public attitudes polarized.

Most China experts in Canada made the case that Canada should do both. But they cautioned that the use of sanctions with business as the lever—say, by stopping the wheat sales—would, as Bernie Frolic argued, "reduce opportunities for engaging China and would likely damage trade without necessarily advancing democracy and human rights."[8] Out of office, Joe Clark wrote in 1996 that Canada had to be able to "accommodate the promotion of both exports and human rights simultaneously."[9]

The Chrétien Decade

The Liberals returned to power in October 1993. Jean Chrétien's government quickly jettisoned its criticisms of the Mulroney government for emphasizing trade at the expense of human rights and ushered in a decade of high-profile commitment to full-scope engagement. Chrétien had extensive experience in China based on various ministerial trips and close family connections with Quebec corporations with major commercial interests in China. China was a priority that he and his government approached assertively. He made his first official visit in November 1994 and five more during his decade as prime minister. He invited several senior Chinese leaders, including Li Peng, a key figure behind the repression in Tiananmen Square, who came to Canada in 1995. The visit produced only sporadic public protests. In 1998 alone, ten different Canadian ministers visited China.

China was back as a foreign policy priority with the trade agenda in command. André Ouellet, the new foreign minister, quickly sought to dispel the Tiananmen hangover. For too long, he stated, "Canada continued to publicly lecture Chinese officials about abuses of human rights ... Other countries have been much quicker to forget Tiananmen Square and come back and re-establish diplomatic, friendly, cordial relations ... The key priority of this government is to create jobs." Two months later he added that "Canadians can't be Boy Scouts" and that "Canada will vigorously pursue [trade] initiatives in a number of countries irrespective of their human rights records."[10] The trade minister, Roy McLaren, underlined that trade sanctions were "a blunt and often ineffective instrument for encouraging reform," indicating that "there is little Canada can do in isolation to persuade China—or any other country accused of abusing its population—to liberalize its human rights or labour rights policies."[11]

The government's policy as outlined in 1994 was to rest on four pillars: economic partnership, sustainable development, peace and security, and human rights combined with the rule of law. Canada would not sacrifice one at the expense of another and committed itself to building an economic partnership with China to create jobs and prosperity in Canada and to benefit the people of China.[12] In a more detailed foreign policy statement, *Canada and the World*, released in February 1995, the government emphasized China's place as a major market and economic player and the value of engaging China in political security discussions and regimes and "in ways to open China to Canadian values."

The most visible push was on trade and investment issues and highlighted by the Team Canada missions organized by Senator Jack Austin that ran annually between 1994 and 2001. The first, in November 1994, featured Prime Minister Chrétien, two cabinet ministers, nine premiers, two territorial leaders, four hundred business leaders, and 1,400 guests for a mammoth banquet in Beijing's Great Hall of the People. The visit concluded with what some called the normalization of relations after Tiananmen and the signing of contracts worth $8.5 billion, including an agreement in principle to purchase two CANDU reactors. In 1990 two-way trade totalled $3.1 billion. By 1995 it was $8 billion, by 2000 $15 billion, and by 2005 $37 billion.

Engagement, Chrétien style, drew criticism from outside and within his own party. The attack did not usually focus on Canadian economic performance but on human rights. Chrétien's simple argument that his government had "never linked trade absolutely to human rights" did not mollify the critics. Nor did his realist argument that, "If I were to say to China, 'We are not dealing with you anymore,' they would say, 'Fine.' They would not feel threatened by Canada strangling them." In 1998 he defended Canada's decision not to link human rights to trade policy and to grant China Most Favoured Nation (MFN) status as it entered the World Trade Organization (WTO), in contrast to the decision of the Clinton administration in Washington.[13]

In 1995, when hosting Li Peng in Montreal, Chrétien again spoke of the "special relationship" between the two countries. Critics were not impressed and retorted that human rights were merely a sideshow for the Chrétien government. Echoing Cold War rhetoric of the 1950s, David Van Praagh claimed that engagement equalled appeasement and that a democratic alliance was needed to stop a China that is "a police state that has not yet cracked, and that seeks to emerge from Asia's chaos as the undisputed lord of 60% of the world's population."[14] The *Globe and Mail* correspondent in Beijing, Miro Cernetig, took aim in a 16 January 1999 column at a policy that was premised on the comforting illusion that the Chinese are "slowly becoming us." Like many Western journalists based in China, he felt that engagement was failing. Rather than learning democracy, China was crushing it. Further, the advantages to Canada were minimal: a huge trade deficit and Chinese firms operating in North America that were stealing secrets. Bob Mills, the Reform Party's foreign affairs critic, criticized the "behind-the-scenes shy approach that doesn't get us a lot of respect from China." Others referred to China as a wolf in sheep's clothing, among the worst abusers of human rights in the world, and the perpetrator of cultural genocide in Tibet. Ross Munro denounced engagement's "pathetic pretensions."

Reflecting the mood of the moment, "Regaining the Moral High Ground in China," a *Globe and Mail* editorial on 1 April 1997 argued that the recent visit of Canada's new foreign minister, Lloyd Axworthy, to China had focused too much on trade and not enough on the environment and human rights. It decried the idea that it was better to make a deal than a point and advocated that Canada protest more aggressively against abuses, offer asylum to dissidents, tie trade to human rights, and impose sanctions. It further advocated bringing the full moral authority of international institutions against China through the U.N. Commission on Human Rights (UNCHR), calling for WTO enforcement of commercial law to make China comply with international standards, and using organizations like APEC—Canada was hosting the Leaders' Summit that year—to draw attention to China's sale of arms to terrorist regimes, its ban on letting Red Cross officials inspect prisons, and its rejection of legal reforms.

Targeting Axworthy was ironic considering that in the public eye and in the corridors of his new department he was regarded as the minister most strongly focused on human rights in Liberal history. He had inaugurated the first Canada-China bilateral dialogue on human rights in 1996 on topics that included the treatment of the dissident Wei Jingsheng, the kidnapping of the Panchen Lama, and female infanticide. He made the decision in April 1997 to halt Canadian support for the annual condemnation of Chinese human rights violations at the U.N. Commission on Human Rights in Geneva in favour of a bilateral and a plurilateral dialogue with China that he and his officials bet could be more effective. He established regular consultations with human rights advocacy groups and supported CIDA's move to a program focused on human rights, good governance, and the rule of law. Axworthy later recalled how he and Chrétien divided responsibilities on China policy. Chrétien concentrated on trade and establishing positive ties with the Chinese regime and Axworthy pushed on human rights issues through "direct bilateral engagement" that involved a visit to China to initiate the bilateral dialogue and provide legal assistance and training.[15]

The bilateral dialogue, formally known as the Canada-China Joint Committee on Human Rights, held nine meetings between July 1997 and November 2005. The plurilateral dialogue, hosted by Canada and Norway, began in 1998 and involved as many as twenty Asian countries. They were augmented by a score of CIDA-funded projects, regular involvement on human rights files by the Political Section of the Canadian Embassy in Beijing, funding of Chinese

NGOs, and Canadian involvement in initiatives of the UNCHR. CIDA funding between 2000 and 2006 went to projects involving the Canadian Bar Association and the Supreme Court of Canada in collaboration with China's Ministry of Justice, the All China Lawyers Association, and the Supreme People's Court on the strengthening of legal and justice systems and judicial reform; the Federation of Canadian Municipalities and the National Development Reform Commission on labour rights; and other projects focused on human rights education and prison reform.

Those who participated in the dialogues were usually not impressed. The meetings were described as ritualistic and hollow. A report commissioned in 2005 by the Department of Foreign Affairs and International Trade (DFAIT), written by Charles Burton, a Brock University academic, and released in 2006, revealed that Chinese participants did not like the "missionary attitude" of the Canadians; the repetitive agenda that included Falun Gong, Tibet, Xinjiang, and the death penalty; and the expectation that all of the discussion about issues and remedies should focus on China alone. One problem was that the organization in control in China was the Ministry of Foreign Affairs not the agencies entrusted to advance human rights. The Chinese complained that it was the wrong forum for responding to specific "cases of concern" that should be handled through other channels, including the Chinese legal system itself.

The report concluded that even though the dialogues produced fatigue and cynicism on both sides they might nevertheless have had some effect in facilitating China's signing of the International Convention on Civil and Political Rights and the International Convention on Economic and Social Rights (with a reservation on Article 8) and changes to the national constitution, including the insertion of the phrase "The State respects and safeguards human rights." They also might have had an influence on several legal developments related to criminal procedure, violence against women, sexual harassment, police conduct, and prison management. There was no impact, the study concluded, in the areas of religious freedom, labour rights, and the rights of ethnic minorities.[16]

Chrétien himself offered a shifting series of explanations for the trade-first approach. One was the appeal to modesty in his famous statement in March 1994 that "I'm not allowed to tell the Premier of Saskatchewan or Quebec what to do. Am I supposed to tell the leader of China what to do?" That November, in Shanghai with the Team Canada mission, he argued that his quiet approach to promoting political freedom in China was the way to be most effective. "Lecturing your hosts," he stated, "would achieve nothing. The way to deal with authoritarian regimes is to offer to help them build a more open system of government." He expressed his conviction that "I'm sure that opening of the market, the opening of these countries to outsiders coming with our values and traditions will help a lot."[17]

The warm tone of his remarks paralleled the substance. In November 1997 during an official visit of President Jiang Zemin to Toronto, Chrétien stated that "friendship and understanding remain at the heart of the Canada-China relationship" and that it was essential to engage China constructively. He raised human rights issues as important to Canadians and a source of his own country's strength. He spoke of assisting China with a new legal framework and judicial training. A year later in Beijing at a meeting of the Canada-China Business Council attended by Premier Zhu Rongji, he stated that Canada "will stand by China as it continues its reform and strengthen and broaden our cooperation and partnership to meet the challenges of the new century." He recommended addressing differences "openly and frankly. Not in the spirit of disrespect, but in the belief that such honesty makes real friendships stronger."

The government did find ways to support the human rights dialogues, criminal law reform, the legal aid system, training for senior judges, research projects on topics including international organizations and women's law, collaborations on public sector reforms, and church visits focused on religious practice. In early 1998 Chrétien and President Jiang announced a new Canada-China Legislative Association, headed on the Canadian side by Senator Jack Austin. The shift from the customary nomenclature of "Parliamentary Associations" was required to overcome the objections of Bill Blaikie, a New Democratic Party (NDP) MP, who felt that China did not have a real "parliament."

Chrétien's fullest statement of Canada's human rights agenda was spelled out in a February 2001 speech to the East China University of Politics and Law.

> The rule of law is about more than just a dry set of rules. The rules themselves reflect fundamental values of right conduct. The Canadian experience, and that of countries around the world, is that these values, and the rights that make them specific, are universal. They are endowed equally to all people, everywhere. Not on the basis of any special power or privilege, but purely and simply because they have been given the gift of life. That is why we call them human rights. And they not only protect people from abuse. They empower them to contribute fully and creatively to building a stronger society. Canada believes that frank discussion among nations about human rights can foster wider respect for and entrenchment of those rights. While circumstances and experiences may vary from nation to nation, we all share a sense of what is just, what is right.

He recalled that he had been the minister of justice when the Trudeau government entrenched the Charter of Rights and Freedoms in the Canadian constitution, one of his proudest achievements in public life. Canada would promote civil society and community activism in China, convene a human rights conference at the Chinese Academy of Social Sciences, and fund a legal aid centre. Out of the public eye his officials negotiated the release and transfer to Canada of several dissident leaders.

Chrétien and his ministers also offered another line of argument tied directly to the remarkable economic and social changes occurring in the 1990s as China emerged as the shop floor of the world. China's economic opening would inevitably, if not immediately and not in linear fashion, bring with it political and social change. Social change was already readily apparent. Demonstrating political change was rather more difficult, and making the case that this was facilitated by outside pressure, including from Canada, more difficult still. Raymond Chan, the secretary of state for Asia Pacific and earlier a democracy and human rights advocate at the time of Tiananmen Square, took on the issue directly. In a June 1996 speech in the House of Commons he claimed that "systematic and wide ranging contact leads to calls for greater openness and freedom. Trade reduces isolationism. Trade expands the scope of international law and generates the growth required to sustain social change and development. A society that depends little on trade and international investment is not open to the inflow of ideas and values … [T]here have been significant human rights improvements in the everyday lives of ordinary Chinese since 1989."[18]

On another front, the Chrétien government actively supported intensive dialogue with China on matters of regional and global security. Some of this was conducted at the level of formal discussions among leaders and officials. The government also encouraged and funded, as had the Progressive Conservatives during Clark's period as foreign minister, several "track-two" mechanisms for bilateral and regional dialogue with Chinese think tanks, universities, and ministries. A combination of support from the political level and funding, guidance, and participation from the bureaucratic side provided the foundation for dozens of initiatives. The topics ranged from managing potential conflicts in the South China Sea to regional security in northeast Asia and the broader Asia Pacific region, the weaponization of space, human security and the Responsibility to Protect, the environment, and climate change. Sometimes things clicked, producing results that were constructive and tangible. A team of Canadian academics, working in collaboration with DFAIT and Chinese research institutes, the Ministry of Foreign Affairs, and the People's Liberation Army, was able to facilitate the drafting of the government's "New Security Concept" in 1997 that developed a rationale and concepts for Chinese participation in regional security processes. China's socialization into the norms and rules of regional and global processes was incomplete, but China had become, in the words of one American observer, "a born again believer" in the value of multilateral institutions.[19] No country was more active or focused in facilitating that rebirth than Canada.

The final months of Chrétien's leadership brought a spate of announcements about new bilateral agreements on climate change, development cooperation, cooperation with the National People's

Congress, programs for child and maternal health in West China, sustainable agriculture, and protection of Yunnan's ecosystem.

Chinese Reactions

However divided the views at home, the Chrétien approach was well received in China. Just as Canada had been a first mover in diplomatic recognition of China in 1970, it was an important partner in re-legitimating the Chinese state internationally after Tiananmen under both the Mulroney and Chrétien governments. The Chinese leadership was appreciative. During Chrétien's visit to Beijing in 1998, Premier Zhu Rongji spoke frankly about the long-term need for democratic change in China. In December 2003 Premier Wen Jiabao met Jean Chrétien in Ottawa. The Ministry of Foreign Affairs website in Beijing noted that "The Sino-Canadian relationship should become an exalted example of a long-term friendship and cooperation between countries of different social systems and different development levels." Wen proposed contacts and exchanges at all levels including a ministerial coordinating mechanism; energy, environment, communication, and finance; science, technology, education, and culture; and co-operation in multilateral organizations. Deals were announced for further potash and wheat sales. And Wen recommended that the two countries establish stronger links at the vice-ministerial level focused on Sino-Canadian relations and coordination of positions on major international issues.

The friendship theme was important. In 2003 President Jiang Zemin referred to departed Canadian Prime Minister Chrétien as his *lao pengyou* or old friend. Even more strikingly, Premier Zhu Rongji stated at a Canada-China Business Council meeting in 1998 that "Canada is China's best friend in the world." This was more than maotai-infused banquet hyperbole. Many officials, politicians, and academics believed that they had the ears of their Chinese counterparts in private discussions and that there was a wellspring of empathy and trust that had emerged during a period of intensive interaction. Beyond personal relations nurtured over thirty years,

Canadians presented themselves and were viewed in what Jeremy Paltiel has described as a combination of non-threatening and non-hostile, a potential partner rather than a rival, open-minded, high in international prestige and respectability, a member of prestigious international clubs, and a "low-profile reference model" for China's political and social modernization.[20]

The invisible hand of economic opening and the more visible one of China's increasingly active participation in international institutions were stronger than their critics acknowledged. China's constructive interaction with the outside world and its emergence as what André Ouellet once described as a "responsible global citizen" were a dramatic departure from its international role two decades earlier. Results could be seen in policy areas ranging from trade and the WTO to regional institutions including APEC and the ASEAN Regional Forum. And they could also be seen in popular fashion, consumer habits, and social change on an enormous scale.

Martin and the Strategic Partnership

When Paul Martin, Jr, replaced Jean Chrétien as leader of the Liberal Party and prime minister in December 2003, engagement remained the high policy of his government, though this time with a twenty-first-century twist that went well beyond two-way trade and moved into the dynamic world of global supply chains and international financial governance. Martin had made several visits to China for business and governmental purposes. By the time he became prime minister, the China that his father had tried so urgently to get into the United Nations had emerged not just as the shop floor of the world, a low-cost manufacturer, and a major consumer of commodities but as an essential player in regional production networks and global value chains. By 2004 China was the second largest trading partner of both Canada and the United States, had amassed major foreign reserves, and was the leading foreign purchaser of U.S. treasuries. Ideas were big and obstacles perceived to be few. Martin's minister of trade, Roy McLaren, made the case for negotiating a Canada-China free trade agreement and an investment agreement. In the list of problems to be overcome, public resistance was not included.[21]

One element of trade promotion was an ambitious plan to upgrade west-coast transportation infrastructure to move goods more efficiently between Asia and North America, China being a key part of the plan. The Pacific Gateway strategy called for major investments by the federal and provincial governments in British Columbia and Alberta to coordinate and expand infrastructure projects. The concept was popular on both sides of the Pacific. Martin was presented with a poem by Li Zhaoxing, China's foreign minister, that captured the heady mood of the moment.

> From Fragrant Hill in Beijing to Vancouver, the maples rule
> The sun dawns on the same crimson landscape, fiery and full.
> Let's walk through the Gateway toward the future together.

Martin's second shift of emphasis was the active pursuit of China as a core member in the G20 process, the successor to the L20 meetings of finance ministers that he had done so much to catalyse. The G20 came to life in the fall of 1999 and focused on ministers of finance from nineteen countries plus the European Union (EU). A supplement and potential successor to the G7/8, it was explicitly constructed to reflect the new economic power and political significance of emerging economies, China's chief among them. The world did not just need to bring China more deeply into existing international institutions, it needed to build new ones with China as a founding member.

During his first official visit to China in January 2005, Martin observed that the international power structure was shifting and that China was emerging with an "increasingly pivotal role on the world stage." He emphasized the comprehensive strength of China as a "major power in all its facets," and, echoing his father's aspiration forty years earlier, the need to adjust the international system to accommodate this centrality.

> Canada welcomes this. We seek to enhance our engagement with China—to foster a real partnership that comprises not just economic

pursuits, but also the global political agenda: public health, environmental issues, human rights, and culture. In essence, we strive to more closely connect our two nations—encouraging the two-way flow of capital, goods and services, while at the same time expanding our dialogue, our exchange of ideas and beliefs. For that is how friendships are deepened and the world made stronger.[22]

Martin's aim was "to build a partnership that embraces the complexity and growing influence of 21st century China." He addressed with his counterparts issues of global security, global warming, the Korean peninsula, the United Nations, the ASEAN Regional Forum and APEC. He made the case for the reform of international institutions, a "New Multilateralism" in which China would be central to its success, and the need for a new financial architecture. His joint statement with Premier Wen spoke of the value of regular bilateral consultations under the aegis of multilateral institutions. On bilateral issues, he made what proved to be a premature announcement about China's intent to award Approved Destination Status to Canada to boost tourism, and conveyed a letter expressing concern about ten individuals in Chinese jails.

At home, the operational approach was "whole of government." Martin encouraged every cabinet minister to visit China and concluded an agreement with Wen to elevate the Strategic Working Groups created in 2001 to the deputy minister level. They were tasked to look at ways to deepen the relationship in multilateral cooperation, natural resources, trade, investment, culture, and science, and to conduct a policy dialogue on human rights and domestic governance.

Deep engagement took on a further dimension during the return visit to Canada of President Hu Jintao in September 2005. The two countries agreed to upgrade the relationship to a strategic partnership. The term was new to Canadians but a category familiar to the Chinese, who in official terms had earlier referred to the relationship as a "trans-century comprehensive partnership." From the Chinese perspective the upgrade reflected "long-term positive relations, connections across a variety of sectors, and the absence of any strategic conflicts." President Hu was reported in the Chinese press as saying, "Thanks to our joint efforts, Canada-China economic ties have evolved from small, simple-item commodity trade into all-dimensional cooperation covering trade in commodity and services, capital flows and personnel exchanges."[23]

The specific ingredients of the strategic partnership included seven new agreements in the areas of transportation, food safety, health sciences, and nuclear energy, and a joint declaration on science and technology that included a program of collaborative research on climate change and sustainable energy. Ottawa signalled not only an interest in a deeper commercial relationship and openness to Chinese investment but a willingness to open the Canadian energy sector to Chinese investment on a commercial basis rather than as a matter of national security. (A month earlier, CNOOC had withdrawn an offer to purchase the U.S. oil company Unocal Corporation for $18.5 billion because of political criticism and national security concerns raised in Congress.) Canada and China agreed to consult closely on issues arising in multilateral institutions including the G20 and the United Nations. There were initial discussions about the possibility of creating a formal linkage between the Liberal Party of Canada and the Chinese Communist Party (CCP) along the lines already established between the CCP and parties in several Western democracies. And Martin spoke privately with his visitor about the situations of ten political dissidents in China and the situation in Tibet.

The strategic partnership was far from monogamous. China had ten other strategic partnerships at the time and a year later would set up something similar with the EU. By 2010 it would have twenty-five. But in many ways it was the high-water mark of a thirty-five-year journey featuring warm and deepening interactions, a dynamic commercial agenda, vastly increased human flows, largely successful management of bilateral irritants, and respect for China's core interests. The tone was frank and constructive in a search for possibilities rather than confrontation. It combined a nascent multilateral dimension with a well-elaborated bilateral one, both premised on the idea that China had emerged as a pivotal global force with implications far beyond the old bilateral relationship. Economically, it stretched the agenda with the hint that energy would be a major new dimension; in the area of human rights it focused on small but concrete steps using the instruments of quiet diplomacy and capacity building.

The "strategic" dimension of the strategic partnership was largely implicit. While wanting to bring China in on the ground floor of a new financial architecture, the Martin government only hinted at the political and security implications of China's rise and the shifting balance of power coming in its wake. There were few public comments by the government at senior levels about growing Chinese military capacity, U.S.-China relations, or Chinese positions on specific regional and global issues. As other countries began debating their strategic options, Ottawa was watchful but largely silent, focusing instead on a commercial agenda and on building multilateral institutions.

The issues that continued to rankle were human rights and democratization. Martin's foreign minister, Bill Graham, laid out the government's approach in April 2004, arguing that since 1996 "Canada has pursued a policy of engagement with China on human rights and governance issues in the belief that engagement is more effective than isolation in bringing about the improvements we seek. Accordingly, we raise human rights consistently at all levels as a major bilateral issue, with some notable results on both the policy level and in individual cases." He reiterated all of the activities set up in the Chrétien era for dialogue and capacity building and special attention to promoting freedom of expression, religion, and assembly, minority rights, and individual consular cases. The aim of the CIDA programs "was not to give charity, but to influence China's transformation in ways compatible with Canadian values and interests, and with what we believe to be the best interests of the Chinese people."[24] CIDA added a new project on migrant rights. When announcing it, Pierre Pettigrew returned to an old argument: "Canada is concerned about the human rights situation in China, and we believe engagement rather than isolation represents the best means to achieve improvements over time."[25]

The trade versus human rights debate refused to die. Tom Axworthy, a former principal secretary to Pierre Trudeau and later chair of the board of the Asia Pacific Foundation of Canada, strongly opposed the attempt by China Minmetals corporation to purchase a Canadian company, arguing that China should not be allowed "to own the assets of our free society until China itself joins the community of the free." He described Hu Jintao as "presiding over an economy inspired by Adam Smith and a party structure borrowed from Joseph Stalin" and made the case that "Getting along with the Communist Party should never mean going along with its worst practices." The next year, he wrote in the *Toronto Star* that China had a major banking crisis: "For the Communist party, the economic doomsday clock is at a quarter to 12 … Engage, but never kowtow."[26]

Business leaders active in China continued to make the argument that Canada should promote human rights through more business. Stanley Hartt lauded the "curative properties of trade and economic liberalization." The bait of trade and the incentive of self-interest in integrating into the world economy would lead China to open and liberalize politically as well. Accordingly, Chinese investment in Canada should not be evaluated on the basis of China's internal political and social policies but on the bet that within a decade China would be "a much-reformed society." Closer economic ties would increase prosperity and human rights in both countries.[27] It was a busy autumn of 2005, with the Canadian Council of Chief Executives sending a delegation of seventeen CEOs to accompany three Canadian ministers and several provincial leaders active in China.

The ambivalence to China—two different conceptions of China warring in the bosom of a single newspaper—was encapsulated in a special edition of the *Globe and Mail* on 23 October 2004 on "China Rising" that began with the lead in Chinese characters: "If you can't read these words, better start brushing up. A profound global shift has begun, one that occurs once every few lifetimes. Don't be left behind." Other headlines read: "Get Ready for China's Century," "Will China Join the Culture Club or Wield It?," "Wenzhou: Capitalism Unbound," "10 Things the Chinese Do Far Better Than We Do," "Low Wages, Cruel Bosses, No Rights," "Flexing Its Military Muscle," "Tibet: In the Crosshairs and at a Crossroads," "Rural Poor Increasingly Marginalized by Galloping Capitalism,"

"Diaspora Forms 'Bamboo' Supply Chain," "How Democracy Would Help China," "The Art of Sealing the Deal in Canton," "Why Canada Can't Afford to Get Left Behind," and "Balancing Commerce and Rights." Howard Balloch, a former Canadian ambassador to China, made the case that China is "fundamentally changing our world." One journalist wrote that it was essential to square business and ethics by pushing China to improve the rule of law, promote workers' rights, encourage corporate social responsibility, increase transparency and honesty, and end corruption. A year later the *Globe and Mail*'s "China Rising 2—Are We Missing the Boat?" was about economic opportunities. Trade was increasing, but only a few were pointing out that, relative to other countries, Canada was falling behind.[28]

Not everyone was impressed or convinced by Prime Minister Martin's claim that China was making progress. Geoffrey York referred in the *Globe and Mail* to the "mundane predictability of the ritualized debate on human rights in China." The *National Post* published stories that spoke of "coddling communists" and Chinese espionage. The *Winnipeg Free Press* proclaimed, "In the 19th century we built a railroad on the backs of Chinese coolies. In the 21st century, we will build a trading empire on the backs of Chinese dissidents."[29]

In the House of Commons, NDP leader Jack Layton argued in October 2005 that the government should use expanded trade as a lever to gain Chinese concessions on human rights and the environment. Conservative MP Jim Abbott pressed ahead with a private member's bill advocating a new Taiwan Affairs Act, Bill C-357, and hearings opened in 2004. Earlier, Conservative foreign affairs critic and former head of the Reform Party Stockwell Day claimed in the *Toronto Star* that it was in the "enlightened national interest of Canadians and the natural rights of freedom-seeking people everywhere" to recognize Taiwan, Canada's "fellow democracy and strategic ally" in international organizations, and a few months later he protested that "it's absolutely inappropriate for mainland Communist China to be threatening democratic Taiwan."[30] Several of Day's speeches in the House also indicated a strong desire for Canada's political disengagement from China on the basis of its poor human rights record and persecution of Christians, Falun Gong adherents, and investigative journalists. He co-sponsored a motion (M-236) in 2002 that urged the Chrétien government to pressure the Chinese government to free imprisoned Falun Gong practitioners with Canadian family ties.

Conservative Party leader Stephen Harper did not address China policy head on but laid down markers that fused morality, power politics, and conservative values. Speaking at a Civitas Society event in April 2003, he stated that,

> The emerging debates on foreign affairs should be fought on moral grounds. Current challenges in dealing with terrorism and its sponsors, as well as the emerging debate on the goals of the United States as the sole superpower, will be well served by conservative insights on preserving historic values and moral insights on right and wrong ... Conservatives must make the moral stand, with our allies, in favour of the fundamental values of society, including democracy, free enterprise, and individual freedom. This moral stand should not just give us the right to stand with our allies, but the duty to do so and the responsibility to put "hard power" behind our international commitments.[31]

Later, in January 2006, he emphasized the importance of the protection and promotion of religious freedom, praising the Dalai Lama as "the champion of peace and pluralism and a hero in defending religious liberty."[32]

Jason Kenney served as a senior member of the Parliamentary Friends of Tibet and of another leading Tibetan activist group, the Canada Tibetan Committee. In April 2004, he recommended to the House of Commons that the Martin government grant honorary Canadian citizenship to the Dalai Lama. In January 2005, while accompanying Prime Minister Martin's delegation to China, he made a high-profile visit to the home of Zhao Ziyang, who had died the week before. Zhao was the former premier who had spoken to Parliament during his 1984 visit and had later fallen into disfavour in Beijing for recommending compromise with the student protestors in Tiananmen Square. Kenney was stopped by security officers outside Zhao's compound but had brought a CTV film crew with him. At the request of the Chinese authorities, Martin had declined to visit to pay his respects. Kenney spoke to the journalists about Martin's "soft-pedaling of human rights" and "how beholden he is to the brutal Communist leadership in Beijing."[33] He then left immediately for the airport and returned to Canada.

Few then imagined that thirteen months later he would be the parliamentary secretary to newly elected Prime Minister Stephen Harper.

chapter four

Harper's Turn

The rise of human rights and democratic institutions was not a product of a particular culture ... Rather, those values, everywhere, were a response to the emergence of new economies, technologies and institutions ... They are not fire and ice: at most they are yin and yang—entwined parts of one another.
Doug Saunders, "Do China a Favour: Stop Calling Them 'Western Values,'"
Globe and Mail, 24 August 2013

The West is uncertain whether China will be good or bad for the world. The tension will only be resolved when both sides approximate each other's world views and accept that they will never have identical cultural values.
Lee Kuan Yew, "Two Images of China," Forbes.com, 16 June 2008

Stephen Harper's Conservative minority government arrived in Ottawa in February 2006 committed to a new agenda for Canada and a "principled" foreign policy. The 171 words on foreign affairs in its election platform did not mention China, nor did the Conservatives include China on their list of Canada's democratic and economic partners in Asia with whom free trade agreements should be negotiated. But their references to democracy promotion as a key priority and criticism of Liberal policies "that compromised democratic principles to appease dictators, sometimes for the sake of narrow business interests," made clear that China and the China policy of the past were in the cross-hairs of an approach that would emphasize the core Canadian values of freedom, democracy, human rights, the rule of law, free markets, and free trade.[1]

The China policy of the Harper government eventually moved a far distance from where it began in 2006. The U-turn away from its early moralism constituted a major foreign policy reversal that eventually landed it very close to the style and approach of its Liberal and Progressive Conservative predecessors that had culminated in the strategic partnership. Yet it has a foundation in a different view of the world, a different philosophy of government, and a different political base. It also has coincided with China's emergence as a major political and economic player, a dramatic shift in economic priorities in the wake of the 2008 financial crisis, and movement in public attitudes about a global China present on Canadian doorsteps. China policy has become difficult for any government, anywhere; doubly so for one inexperienced in foreign affairs, rooted in a values-based Western univeralism, and averse to big-picture geo-strategic thinking.

Cool Politics, Warm Economics

The Conservatives brought with them strong anti-Communist impulses honed since the missionary period, little ground-level knowledge of living in Asia or Asia policy, a deeper connection to Taiwan than to mainland China or Hong Kong, extensive NGO contacts with exile groups and immigrants harshly critical of China, a values-based world view that drew a sharp distinction between friends and enemies based on their political systems, and a libertarian-infused philosophy of governance that envisioned a "small government" role focused on facilitating transactions rather than building relationships.

There was very little from Conservative think tanks and writers in Canada by way of an Asian agenda for the new government. Books like Roy Rempel's *Dreamland* attacked the previous ideas of Liberal governments about multilateralism, soft power, and human security, while saying very little about China.[2] The playbook, if there was one, was largely the product of home-grown criticisms of China's Communist leaders and ideas about developments in China and a China threat incubated in American neo-conservative think tanks, chief among them the American Enterprise Institute.

The disdain for Liberal foreign policy was palpable, the Liberals' engagement policy towards China a prime target. Within weeks of the Conservatives' taking power, advisers to Prime Minister Harper spoke privately of shifting Canada's focus in Asia from "totalitarian China" to "democratic India." Members of caucus and Cabinet described China as a godless, totalitarian country with nuclear weapons aimed at Canada.

The first phase of policy took the form of what can be described as "cool politics, warm economics." "Warm economics" echoed the emphasis of previous governments on trade promotion. The Conservatives embraced most of the Liberals' Gateway strategy embodied in Bill C-68, the Pacific Gateway Act, and transformed it into the Asia Pacific Gateway and Corridor Initiative. It resisted protectionist pressures to limit Chinese exports, encouraged Chinese investment, though without setting clear guidelines and rules, and opened new trade offices in China as part of a global commerce strategy. Two-way trade expanded, as did Chinese investment in Canada, even though in relative terms the Canadian share of both continued to decline.

"Cool politics" was the innovation. The first public comments about China by the new government came in April when the foreign minister, Peter MacKay, indicated that Canada was "very concerned" about the level of Chinese espionage in Canada. That fall he emphasized that a principled foreign policy meant that China, like other countries, would be viewed through the lens of freedom, democracy, human rights, and the rule of law. Chinese representatives in Ottawa were not able to meet him until June, he did not speak with his Chinese counterpart until September, and he did not travel to China until April 2007. Then he spoke of a "constructive and comprehensive relationship" rather than "engagement" or "strategic partnership," terms Canadian ministers and diplomats were now banned from using. Prime Minister Harper declined at least two early invitations to visit China.

Shortly after coming to office, the Harper government granted asylum to Lu Decheng, one of three dissidents jailed for splashing paint on the portrait of Mao Zedong in Tiananmen Square. In itself this was not unusual, as previous Liberal and Progressive Conservative governments had offered asylum to a stream of dissidents dating back to the 1980s. What was unusual was the publicity given to the decision. More significantly, Prime Minister Harper became personally and publicly involved in the case of Huseyincan Celil, a Canadian citizen of Uyghur origin who was imprisoned by China on charges of terrorism in late 2005. Later the case was raised by Peter MacKay during his May 2007 visit, by Paul Martin during his own visit two weeks later, and then by Maxime Bernier after his appointment as foreign minister in August 2007. En route to an APEC meeting in Hanoi in November 2006, Prime Minister Harper told reporters that confronting China on human rights issues was both right and popular. "I think Canadians want us to promote our trade relations worldwide, and we do that. But I don't think Canadians want us to sell out important Canadian values—our belief in democracy, freedom, human rights. They don't want us to sell out to the almighty dollar." Three months later he again spoke publicly about the Celil case, reminding Chinese officials that they needed to be cautious, considering China's large trade surplus. China cancelled a full bilateral meeting between Harper and Hu in Hanoi, paring it back to a fifteen-minute "fly by." Harper pressed Celil's case, telling reporters after the meeting that "at present, we run a massive trade deficit with China ... The fact of the matter is that neglecting human rights hasn't opened a lot of doors either, so obviously we don't think you get anywhere by short-changing your values."[3] Raising individual cases was not unusual; making their settlement a pre-condition for discussing other matters with Chinese leaders was.

In October 2006 the government publicly responded to a long-standing request from several human rights organizations by postponing the bilateral human rights dialogue with China and tasking the Subcommittee on International Human Rights of the Standing Committee on Foreign Affairs and International Development to hold hearings on China. Its chair, Jason Kenney, told the *Epoch Times* after the first hearing that "the new government intends to address these issues with clarity and in a way that reflects Canadian values ... We can pursue our commercial interests in a thoughtful and businesslike fashion without selling out on belief in human rights and religious freedom." Kenney later described the approach as "principled engagement" in which the Canadian government could articulate its belief in fundamental democratic values while achieving 12 per cent annual increases in exports to China. "You don't have to kowtow in order to get results," he said.[4]

The subcommittee heard mainly from witnesses who described massive human rights violations in China and argued that human rights should be at the heart of Canada-China relations. This went well beyond the older discourse that there should be a balance between trade and human rights. It favoured treating human rights as primary and universal, and doing this in bold and public ways, betting that it would not have any effect on a burgeoning trade relationship. A private draft of the report was circulated in May 2007 but not released publicly. Some of its general ideas, but without explicit reference to China, were rolled into a larger report, "Advancing Canada's Role in International Support for Democratic Development," produced by the Standing Committee on Foreign Affairs and International Development three months later.

Government words and actions came close to crossing red lines with respect to Chinese core interests on sovereignty that had been respected since 1970. In July 2006, a Conservative backbencher tabled a motion offering honorary citizenship to the Dalai Lama. This received unanimous support, and on 9 September the award was made. On 29 October 2007, Prime Minister Harper received the Dalai Lama in his Centre Block office with a Tibetan flag displayed on his desk. The only other time a Canadian prime minister had met the Dalai Lama was when Paul Martin met him 2004 in the residence of the Catholic Archbishop of Ottawa. Individual MPs spoke about the virtues of Taiwanese independence and about self-determination for Tibet. For the first time four cabinet ministers attended Taiwan's 10 October celebration in 2006. In August 2007 the Harper government quietly supported a high-level effort by Tokyo and Washington to boost Taiwan's campaign for entry into the World Health Organization. "It's like our China policy is made in Tibet," a former member of the Harper Cabinet was quoted as saying.[5]

Cool did not mean cold. The government formally maintained its One China Policy, did not make any dramatic overtures to Taiwan, and continued its aid program to China. Ministers began visiting

China in the fall of 2006, starting with the minister of agriculture in October and the minister of natural resources a month later. David Emerson, the minister of international trade, and Jim Flaherty, the minister of finance, followed in January 2007.

The ministerial visits were low-key but welcome in China in a period that was otherwise characterized by snubs, public jousting, and cold-shouldering. During his January 2007 trip, Flaherty spoke of actively working to strengthen the Canada-China relationship, engaging China as a rising economic power, working together on IMF reform, promoting economic freedoms, and recognizing Canada's emerging role as an energy superpower. The visitors, however, continued to stay away from the vocabulary of "friendship," "engagement," and "strategic partnership."

In April 2008, Harper announced that he would not attend the Olympic Games in Beijing, though he insisted that his decision was unrelated to the suppression of protests in Tibet. That same month a Conservative MP from Alberta described China as a modern-day Nazi Germany, linking the Beijing Olympics to the 1936 Olympics in Berlin and comparing Falun Gong to the Jews.[6]

Official Chinese reactions moved from puzzlement to anger. Ambassador Lu Shumin raised concerns in speeches and private meetings throughout the fall and winter of 2006. A parliamentary delegation visiting the National People's Congress in October 2006 was told by their Chinese hosts about an "increase in contradictions" between the two countries related to the increasing number of Canadian parliamentarians visiting Taiwan, the granting of honorary Canadian citizenship to the Dalai Lama, and the perceived tolerance of Canadian authorities towards Falun Gong demonstrators.[7] In response to the awarding of honorary citizenship to the Dalai Lama, the Chinese cancelled the meetings of the Strategic Working Groups scheduled for that fall. In February 2007, He Yafei, China's vice-minister of foreign affairs, stated that "I cannot say Canada is squandering the relationship now, but in practical terms Canada is lagging behind in its relations with China." He indicated that confidence and respect were lacking and that there was "room for improvement," nevertheless offering resumption of the high-level working groups agreed to under the terms of the strategic partnership.[8] Following the warm reception accorded to the Dalai Lama in 2007, the angry rhetoric was ratcheted up: a spokesperson for the Chinese Ministry of Foreign Affairs in Beijing accused Canada of "conniving" with Tibetan "splittists" and described the forty-minute meeting between Harper and the Dalai Lama in the prime minister's office as "disgusting conduct."[9]

In June 2007 a visiting delegation from the National People's Congress led by Lu Congmin took issue with the view that China needs Canada more than Canada needs China and asked that ideology not be allowed to get in the way of good relations. Beijing deliberately postponed the visit of its minister of finance until the fall. China continued to withhold Approved Destination Status (ADS) that had been discussed during the Martin period. Canada's deputy minister of foreign affairs could not secure high-level meetings during his trip to Beijing in November 2007 just after Harper's meeting with the Dalai Lama. The Chinese minister of commerce, Bo Xilai, visited Canada that same month. He had earlier stated that mutual trust was slipping and that relations "have moved backward under Harper." In Ottawa he stated that Canada needed to send strong political signals and re-establish political trust.

In January 2008, Ambassador Lu spoke to the Canada-China Friendship Society meeting in Ottawa about "positive developments and unfortunate setbacks." "At stake is not only exchanges and interaction at the government level," he told the audience. "Nothing undercuts bilateral relations more than the souring impression among the public. And in China the feeling is actually spreading."

The China chill was felt across Ottawa in a variety of ministries and agencies. The "whole-of-government" approach of the Chrétien and Martin periods was on hold. While there were no formal instructions to halt or ramp down interactions with China, bureaucrats felt that new programming was risky. The DFAIT was largely cut out of a policy formulation role and was unable to get Cabinet to approve two versions of a China strategy it had prepared. Ministers as well as diplomats were severely constrained in the messages they could convey or the latitude they enjoyed in interactions with audiences across the country or with Chinese counterparts. The expert community of academics and business leaders with extensive experience in China was no longer involved in policy discussions, which were firmly controlled by Prime Minister Harper and a few in his office. Most of the track-two dialogues with China withered. Not since the first months of the Pierre Trudeau government had foreign policy been more concentrated in so few hands or had diplomats and other experts been more on the outside. The main difference was that in the Trudeau period China was a priority and within a matter of months the circle of decision making and consultations expanded geometrically. The Leninist-like centralization and control of decision and communication in the Harper era were to prove far more durable.

As the public face and most ardent advocate of a hard-line approach to China, Jason Kenney not only disagreed with the approach of prior governments but defended his government's decision not to have Harper attend the 2008 Beijing Olympics, attacking Jean Chrétien and other Liberals as "advancing their own personal financial interests and those of rich and powerful friends."[10] And he stuck with his argument that the approach would not have negative economic consequences for the country or negative electoral ones for the party. He argued in caucus that cool politics was a vote getter in key urban ridings where immigrant communities from China and India would view favourably a hard-line approach focusing on human rights.

By late 2007 it was clear that there were consequences and that the approach had put Canada in a category of one, as almost every other government in the world was approaching engagement with the fervour and techniques the Harper government was abandoning. Ottawa was quickly depleting a reservoir of good will in official quarters in Beijing, stood virtually alone among Western countries, and was beginning to pay a tangible economic price. Academics, business leaders, officials (in private conversations), and much of the media were harshly critical, variously describing the government's approach as aloof, introverted, fraught, confused, perverse, immature, juvenile, wobbly, amateurish, one-dimensional, childish and petulant, a colossal mistake, uncreative destruction, out of sync with allies and friends, and a toxic mix of ignorance, ideology, and certainty. Elite support was limited to a handful of academics, some of the right-wing press, and representatives of several NGOs. While it resonated with some of the Conservative base, there were signs that it was not having the desired effect with ethnic Chinese voters in key urban ridings in Toronto and Vancouver. Provincial leaders were beginning to fill the China gap by planning their own visits and projecting a tone and pushing issues such as ADS that had formerly been the domain of the federal government.

The economic concerns were compelling. Canadian business leaders of all political persuasions were talking about lost deals, lost momentum, and lost opportunities. Two-way trade was increasing in absolute terms but declining relative to that of other countries, including the United States and Australia. It was clear that, however important the American market was to Canada, huge growth opportunities lay elsewhere. In 2007 China exported more to the United States than did Canada. By 2009 China was the largest trading partner of every major country in Asia, including Japan, South Korea, and Taiwan, and was beginning to make massive investments abroad.

The Conservatives had made trade with China a priority as an emerging economy even as it made the Americas its priority geographic focus. Diversification would not become a Conservative catchword until after the financial crisis of 2008; but even earlier, all except the most ideologically blinkered were sensing the shifting centre of economic gravity.

U-Turn: Warm Politics, Hotter Economics

The government had dug itself into a hole and was looking for a ladder to climb out. As early as the fall of 2007 there were hints of what one journalist described as a "more nuanced approach" and a "moderated tone" that focused on economics and energy rather than moralism.[11] The new foreign minister, Maxime Bernier, met the Chinese ambassador within two weeks of being appointed in May 2007 and had his department try to resuscitate the Strategic Working

Groups. Secretary of State Helena Guergis spoke at the University of Alberta in January 2008 about the commitment to "sustained high-level engagement," "results-based cooperation," China as a "top priority for trade and investment," and the need for mutual respect. The word "engagement" was a breakthrough. Later that month, at a G8 meeting in Japan, Harper had a forty-five-minute bilateral meeting with President Hu.

Hotter economics formed part of the government's "Prosperity Agenda for Canadians," and focused on Gateway expansion, diversifying markets, changing the mix of exports, facilitating business, more agreements, and encouraging Chinese investments in a Canada "open for business"—in short, a partial return to the approach and vocabulary of the Mulroney and Chrétien governments.

Canadian and Chinese officials privately discussed ways to improve relations and "rebuild confidence" through a synchronized series of visits leading towards a meeting of heads of government. Key were the trips during 2009 of Minister of Transport John Baird in February, Trade Minister Stockwell Day in April, Foreign Minister Lawrence Cannon in May, and Finance Minister Jim Flaherty again in August along with a delegation that included the governor of the Bank of Canada. The Canadian Armed Forces sent an admiral to observe the Chinese Navy's fleet on the occasion of its sixtieth anniversary. Chinese Foreign Minister Yang Jiechi visited Canada in June 2009. The agendas of these visits were increasingly substantial. Trade Minister Day's visit, in particular, had a major impact on his own thinking and on the development of what he called a "holistic" approach to the relationship. When the Dalai Lama visited Canada in September 2009 he met the governor general but neither the prime minister nor the foreign minister. Ottawa offered to resume the human rights dialogue.

One unmistakable sign that the Conservative approach was tactically shifting was its award of $2.3 million in October 2009 for a "New Look" visitors centre at Norman Bethune House in Gravenhurst, Ontario. The grounds and house had been purchased in 1973 by a federal government intent on finding connections with the Chinese government. At the time, the Trudeau government had to gulp hard when celebrating a Communist internationalist. The Conservative twist, that Bethune represented the Canadian virtues of "humanism and entrepreneurship," demonstrated the plasticity of the Bethune myth and a new-found Conservative pragmatism.

That pragmatism was on full display during the Harper visit to China in December 2009. The trip generated very little publicity in China and began with what many interpreted as a rebuke to Harper by Premier Wen Jiabao for not visiting earlier. Harper departed with an agreement on ADS and concessions on beef and pork exports. The Joint Statement of 3 December anointed the Strategic Working Groups as a leading part of more than forty bilateral consultation mechanisms. The statement recognized "distinct points of view" on human rights and promised more dialogue and exchanges. It also addressed the need for completing a bilateral foreign investment protection treaty. On multilateral issues it spoke to the value of the Six Party Talks focused on the North Korean nuclear weapons program and deeper collaboration on issues before the United Nations, APEC, and the G20, with special mention of global health and climate change. In Shanghai on 4 December, Harper recounted the "shared history" between the two countries, starting with the Diefenbaker wheat sales, and highlighted expanding trade, the Gateway, investment, energy, and collaboration in the context of the Asia Pacific Partnership on Clean Development and Climate and the G20.

> Just as trade is a two-way street, so too is dialogue ... Canada, while far from perfect, is one of the most peaceful, pluralistic and prosperous democracies the world has ever known. To Canadians, these attributes are inseparable, and Canadians of Chinese origin participate as fully in them as any of our citizens. And so, in relations between China and Canada, we will continue to raise issues of freedom and human rights, and be a vocal advocate and an effective partner for human rights reform, just as we pursue the mutually beneficial economic relationship desired by both our countries.[12]

Save for the word "freedom," the speech could have been delivered by any of his recent predecessors.

Travelling with the Harper entourage, John Ibbitson called the visit a tipping point that included a "Damascene conversion to

the importance of Asia" and a "subtle sidestep" that, without dis-
avowing earlier sentiments, moved the Conservative government
into "a new and revitalized relationship with China, while not ac-
knowledging its earlier misdirection, and counting on no one to
notice."[13] The relationship was no longer a consular case or diplomatic incident away from a rupture.

The trip triggered an active period of concluding bilateral agreements that strengthened the infrastructure for bilateral relations,
among them ADS and renewed negotiations on a FIPPA, the conclusion of a complementarities study as a possible precursor to an
eventual free trade agreement, and agreements on Civilian Nuclear
Cooperation and air safety. The embassy in Beijing moved to create
an online e-presence to disseminate information about Canada and
Canadian views that soon proved to be popular, garnering several
hundred thousand followers.

President Hu made a formal visit in June 2010 in advance of the G20
meeting in Toronto. China finally ratified ADS and opened staged access to beef imports. Harper again focused on bilateral commercial
issues and offered a sentimental history of the relationship, focusing
on Progressive Conservative highlights. Most importantly, he spoke
warmly for the first time of "the growing strategic partnership"
and "friendly and productive engagement." The two countries applauded the opening of new representative offices and signed agreements on tourism, economic protection, energy conservation, and
law enforcement. President Hu revisited the friendship tree that he
had planted five years earlier. This time Canada was a human rights
exemplar rather than a model. "Power comes not from arms but from
economic power and the stockpile of moral authority a nation builds
up when it upholds the universal values of freedom, democracy, human rights and the rule of law," stated Harper. "China and Canada
have begun a frank dialogue about these values. Continuing it will
bring us closer together as friends and strategic partners."

On 13 October 2010, at an event celebrating forty years of diplomatic relations, Harper offered a glowing account of his visit to
China, noted thirty ministerial visits to China since 2006, acknowledged that the "global economic centre of gravity moves toward
the Pacific," and spoke of the need for dialogue on the universal

principles of human rights and the rule of law. He fulsomely stated that the "Strategic Partnership … has never been more promising." A day later John Baird reiterated the same points but subtly replaced the word "democracy" with "good governance" and spoke of a strategic partnership that is "comprehensive in nature." In Beijing, Ambassador David Mulroney told an academic audience that "if ever there was a golden period in Canada-China relations it is now."

On 29 June, in the first speech on China and foreign policy after the Conservatives had won a majority government in the May 2011 election, the new minister of foreign affairs, John Baird, emphasized that China is "a clear priority for our government and economy." Stating that the government was committed to "continued and sustained high-level engagement with China" and that the relationship was at "a high water mark," he reminded the Canada-China Business Council audience of the many ministerial visits to China since 2006 and addressed issues related to law enforcement, legal cooperation, impediments to business, air transport, tourism, education, people-to-people engagement, and commercial relations. Upbeat in tone, he ended with an unprecedented request for advice on further steps that could be taken to upgrade the relationship.[14] In later comments he referred to China as a friend, strategic partner, and ally.[15] He and the government were apparently pleased by the extradition of Lai Changxing to China after a protracted refugee claim that had begun more than a decade earlier. Lai, accused of corruption and bribery in China, was returned to China a day after Baird's visit ended. Baird left no doubt that the Harper government was not unhappy to see Lai, a "white collar fraudster," returned home. Many inferred a clear link between the settlement of the Lai case and the granting of ADS a few months earlier. Meantime, Chinese diplomats declined to comment on the remarks by the head of the Canadian Security and Intelligence Service that several Canadian municipal and provincial officials had fallen under the sway of a foreign government that many inferred was China. Harper did not replace the director but neither did he use the occasion as an opportunity to comment on Chinese espionage.

When Prime Minister Harper visited China a second time, in February 2012, he made a special trip to Chongqing to see Bo Xilai, the son of a major personage in the Communist Party who was well connected to Canada and a rising star in the Party, though very soon to fall from grace. Harper was playing the game of cultivating high-level connections, the final ingredient of the playbook that Trudeau had written. In Guangzhou, Harper stated that "China has shown the world how to make poor people rich, through frugality and diligence, and of course, the application of market economics." He continued, "The world is a better place for a China that favours free trade over protectionism, for a China that plays the constructive role it did at last year's G20, and for a China whose people will value social and political progress as much as its economic growth."[16]

Where Trudeau had taken beavers and operating equipment from Norman Bethune's Montreal surgery as gifts in his 1973 visit, and Governor General Adrienne Clarkson had received the friendship tree planted by President Hu outside Rideau Hall in September 2005, and Paul Martin a Gateway poem, it was Stephen Harper who received the pandas that arrived in March 2013. As uncomfortable as Harper looked when he was photographed with two of the animals on his knee during his December 2012 visit, in an unmistakeable symbol of the importance of the relationship, he met their larger cousins, Da Mao and Er Shun, in person when they landed at the Toronto airport.

With bilateral relations again on a familiar if somewhat precarious footing, the international and multilateral dimensions of those relations began to appear in Canadian statements. For example, during President Hu's visit to Canada in 2010 for a state visit preceding the G20 meetings in Toronto, Harper expressed his desire to work with Hu in seeking a new consensus on international financial regulation, economic stability, a cleaner and safer environment, improved health and security in the developing world, and effective international action against terrorists and rogue states. Those close to Harper have observed that Harper's view of the significance of China as a global power had undergone a dramatic change during the G20 meeting in Pittsburgh three years earlier when he was heard to remark that China and the United States were the two key countries in the room. The economic crisis of 2008 had changed the world economic scene.

Chinese Ambassador Zhang Junsai described relations in the summer of 2011 as "very warm" and the result of the Harper government's deeper exposure to international affairs.[17] When Harper spoke with Premier Wen in the Great Hall of the People, he praised "a strategic partnership based on respect and admiration." Wen replied that the visit "had opened a new page in our bilateral relationship."[18] When Harper met for a third time with the Dalai Lama on 27 April 2012, it was for a "private courtesy meeting" with a spiritual leader and an honorary Canadian. In another ironic twist, he was criticized by NDP MPs for not meeting with the Dalai Lama publicly.

By 2012 the Conservatives had completed a remarkable policy reversal—never explained or elaborated by senior government leaders. Former officials have rightly pointed to the government's distaste for grand pronouncements and strategic planning. They also claim that there has been a systematic plan in play since 2009 to rebuild the relationship from the ground up through a series of bilateral agreements on trade offices, FIPPA, and ADS that have, in combination, provided a new substructure, a new plumbing, for the relationship. The plan could be deduced from actions.

Several other forces have also been in play. There had been overwhelming support from business and expert communities for the approach to China by earlier governments that the Harper government had initially spurned. Over time, as Harper and his senior ministers developed first-hand knowledge of China, they were generally impressed and occasionally awestruck. Senior Chinese officials played a patient hand in reacting to Ottawa. Meanwhile, Harper had seen Chinese influence and power in play at several international meetings. Cool politics had not brought the hoped-for electoral advantage with voters of Chinese descent in the key urban ridings targeted by the Conservatives, though they won several of those ridings for other reasons. And the ground-level realities in the relationship had shifted dramatically, especially after the economic crisis of 2008–9 that seemed to accelerate the comparative significance of global China.

In many respects the high policy of engagement was back to where the Martin government had left it in 2005: an economic agenda pushed aggressively; frequent and cordial high-level visits; frequent mention of Canadian values and human rights; quiet management of sensitive cases; and respect for Chinese sensitivities on Tibet, Taiwan, and sovereignty issues.

In other respects, engagement with Conservative characteristics had staked out different ground. Few if any big ideas are in play. Nothing in Conservative foreign policy outlines an overarching strategy related to world order, China's place in it, and a comprehensive agenda of priorities. There is little emphasis on the geopolitical dimensions of China's rise and a visible allergy to framing any Canadian role as a bridge or middle power in facilitating China's emergence as a responsible international actor. Instead, the emphasis is on managing and facilitating a transactional relationship focused on trade and investment. Professionals and experts are not as disdained as in 2006, but decision making remains firmly in the hands of Prime Minister Harper. The consultative processes initially envisioned for the Gateway initiatives and strategic partnership disappeared. When Harper visited China in 2012 he took a small number of MPs and energy executives with him but no one from the opposition parties or from environmental or First Nations groups. Though China-related activities have not been cut as substantially as other parts of DFAIT, and new resources have gone into trade positions in China, the funding for programming, dialogues, and new initiatives has shrunk perceptibly.

Engagement has a different hue in part because of the leadership style and priorities of the Harper government. It also reflects a different political base and world view. Distrust of China and its Communist leaders has deep roots. A significant number of the caucus and Cabinet, especially those from the Reform/Alliance side of the party, continue to see China as godless, totalitarian, a security threat, and ruled by an illegitimate and morally unacceptable government.

The mantra of freedom, democracy, human rights, and the rule of law is the rhetorical foundation but is largely unaccompanied by major programming and initiatives to improve on the achievements of earlier governments in advancing these principles. The contradiction at the heart of the Conservative approach is that it is based on firm and unshakeable principles that implicitly demand profound political and social change in China before it can be treated as a full equal. At the same time the Conservatives have done considerably less than preceding governments to strengthen mechanisms for attempting to influence or proactively shape China's domestic and foreign affairs, a partial exception being occasional statements about matters of religious freedom coming from the newly created Office of Religious Freedom.

The trust factor that was an important ingredient of engagement strategies starting with Trudeau is substantially higher than it was during the period of "cool politics, warm economics." But in Conservative Ottawa, engagement remains partial and conditional with an overwhelming emphasis on commercial priorities. The Conservative paradox is that the principles of freedom, democracy, human rights, and the rule of law that were the foundations of its policy in 2006 continue to resonate with its political base even as they are not seriously pursued in practice.

Public Anxieties

The Harper government's policy reversal was recognized and applauded by academics and business associations, including the Canadian Council of Chief Executives, the Canada-China Business Council, and most of the diplomatic service. Yet the anxieties lurking beneath the earlier hard-line approach grew in the minds of many Canadians and some influential political figures. The negativity about China reflected in public reactions to the sale of Nexen to CNOOC in 2012 was shared and in some ways amplified, sometimes inadvertently, sometimes passionately, by Conservative political figures.

Polls dating back to the Cold War underline the fact that a significant number of Canadians have never been comfortable with the People's Republic of China. In 1949 only 40 per cent of Canadians supported diplomatic recognition. Even on the eve of recognition in 1969 only 52 per cent were in support. The number opposed was never less than 28 per cent and was at its high point of 44 per cent just before the Diefenbaker wheat sales in 1960.[19]

In Canada, as elsewhere, contemporary China generates two reactions, as seen in a range of international surveys, most significantly the ones conducted by the Asia Pacific Foundation of Canada since 2004.[20] The first reaction is that China is big, important, and getting more so. The second is a blend of uncertainty, anxiety, and fear—leavened by a sense of opportunity—about what this portends. A majority of Canadians believe that Chinese influence in the world will surpass American influence within a decade, up to 67 per cent in 2012. Canadians also consistently overestimate the extent of existing trade with China and Asia, frequently by a factor of two or three. A little over half now see it as an economic opportunity rather than an economic threat. Almost half favour a free trade agreement.

Yet in 2013 almost three times as many Canadians have a cold or unfavourable view of China as have a warm or favourable one. China is consistently seen by a significant number of Canadians as corrupt, authoritarian, and threatening. Concern about China's growing military power is significant, and fewer than one in five Canadians are in favour of allowing a state-controlled company from China to buy a controlling stake in a major Canadian company.

A majority of Canadians continue to believe that human rights and democracy are vital for Canada and want the Canadian government to focus on these issues in its relations with Asian countries. Two-thirds believe it is possible to do business in China while at the same time raising human rights concerns; a little more than half believe that human rights promotion should be a major priority of the Canadian government in Asia, and a little less than half believe the same about democracy promotion. At the same time six in ten believe that Canada should take action on human rights at home before preaching to Asians.

The national debate in 2012 about the CNOOC purchase of Nexen revealed widespread negativity and distrust about the limits of the strategic partnership and deeper economic engagement with China. Several polls indicated that almost three-quarters of Canadians opposed the takeover even as it was strongly supported by the Alberta government, the Nexen board and shareholders, and the majority of investment experts. The arguments against the sale fell into two categories. The first focused on the risks associated with dealing with state-owned enterprises (SOEs) in general, a view that they were less profitable than private sector competitors, the specifics of the deal, the need to protect Canadian champions in the energy sector, the enforceability and scope of the undertakings promised by CNOOC, the desire for reciprocity in opening doors for Canadian business opportunities in China, anxiety about perceived connections between Chinese SOEs and intelligence gathering, industrial espionage, and the Chinese military. Some predicted a domino effect with the CNOOC investment as the first wave in a series of Chinese investments that would amount to a takeover of the Canadian energy sector. Free-market ideology and economic nationalism conjoined in an unlikely if potent combination.

The second category focused on China itself. SOEs like CNOOC were criticized for alleged connections to Chinese intelligence and espionage, the Chinese military, and the Chinese Communist Party (CCP)—all striving for world domination. The result was a popular narrative that doing business with Chinese SOEs meant dealing with the Chinese state, that the Chinese state was controlled by the CCP, and that the state oppressed its people and violated their basic human rights.

The same kinds of arguments and sentiments surfaced in sharp public reactions to the signing of the FIPPA that was concluded in October 2012 after fourteen years of on-again, off-again negotiations. Concerns focused on a potential Huahui investment in a Canadian technology company and the importing of Chinese workers in the mining sector. Underlying some of the opposition were broad anxieties about the environmental risks of direct export of Canadian energy to Asia from west-coast ports.

The approval of both the Nexen sale and the FIPPA by the Harper government produced internal criticism within caucus, the Cabinet, and the Conservative base, as well as in the wider public. Ministers heard concerns about the transactions themselves, as well as objections to China's trafficking in animal parts and ivory, anger over shark fin soup, and concerns about product safety, China's military build-up, and its assertive approach to its maritime borders, including in the South China Sea.

Several Conservative MPs, including Harold Albrecht, Russ Hiebert, and LaVar Payne, expressed their concerns publicly. One Albertan MP, James Bezan, opposed the Nexen sale on the grounds that "The Communist Chinese government continues to fail to grant even the most basic of human freedoms to its citizens, as they strip away their national wealth to invest around the world. CNOOC's past possible human rights abuses and failure to report oil spills is something I am also very concerned about."[21] There has never been unanimity of thinking about China in any Canadian political party, but in this case the opposition within the Conservative party threatened for the first time to disrupt the control of Prime Minister Harper on a key foreign policy issue.

This criticism built on earlier condemnations of China that were tied to the suppression of the Falun Gong movement and Chinese policies in Tibet. David Kilgour and David Matas in May 2008 described China as a tyranny, totalitarian, repressive, financier of genocide in Darfur, supplier of arms to brutal regimes, harvester of Falun Gong organs, agent of repression in Tibet, user of the death penalty, operator of labour camps, abuser of human rights lawyers, and led by a Communist regime that "has killed more innocents than Nazi Germany and Stalinist Russia combined," is unaccountable to its people for events including Tiananmen Square, and controls the legal system.[22] Lawrence Solomon wrote in the *Financial Post* during Harper's trip to China in February 2012 that President Hu Jintao "stands atop a vast chaos, a seething, heaving economy of plunderers that keeps the plundered at bay through an army of spies and thugs, of thieves that pirate the West's designs and innovations, and of military adventurers who threaten to seize property and resources from nearly all its neighbours ... China today is more repressive than at any time since the Tiananmen crackdown in 1989."[23] Other columnists in the *Financial Post* and in the *Ottawa Citizen* criticized the Harper government for taking the strategic partnership too seriously as a mercenary romance, for moral blindness, and for selling Canada's soul to an unsavoury regime.[24]

A further element was concern about Chinese espionage in Canada. Harper himself, as leader of the opposition, had raised concerns about "a thousand Chinese spies" who were allegedly operating in Canada. Peter MacKay referred to this in March 2006 not long after being appointed minister of defence. Jim Judd, director of the Canadian Security and Intelligence Service, told a Senate committee in April 2007 that almost half of the foreign intelligence agents operating in Canada were from China, and in June 2010 his successor, Richard Fadden, stated publicly that a number of municipal and provincial officials were under the influence of a foreign government, the implication being that the country was China.

Preston Manning opposed the Nexen sale, in part on the grounds that it was unpopular with most Canadians, while also providing a principled case against it. Noting that Canada was anxious to expand trade with China, he observed that the "Communist government practices and promotes a version of capitalism and 'democracy' unacceptable to many Canadians." He framed the sale as part of a "deadly serious political competition with China" that "pits the well-developed Chinese Communist ideology of state-controlled capitalism and state-directed 'democracy' against the older Western ideology of market-driven capitalism and citizen-directed democracy. This competition is especially keen in the developing countries where the West and China compete for resources." The West, he added, "appears to be losing the competition."[25]

Some of this Manichean logic was echoed in an essay by the former Canadian ambassador to China, David Mulroney, a skilled player in putting in place the grid of new agreements that were cornerstones of the later Harper approach to China. Without offering a judgment on whether the Nexen sale should be approved, he stated that the discussion brought into focus the "difficult choices that come with engaging a country that is fundamentally unlike ours and whose objectives and policy directions are hard to follow." The essay made the balanced case for trying harder to understand China, "warts and all," and for bringing patience, competence, and confidence to "managing our engagement with a dynamic, perplexing and increasingly important partner."[26]

On 7 December 2012 the Harper government approved the Nexen sale, subject to undertakings privately agreed with CNOOC and with new guidelines that would substantially restrict the capacity of any SOE to make majority-ownership purchases in future in the oil sands except under "exceptional circumstances." The government's statement emphasized that investments by SOEs would be looked at differently because their "larger purposes may well go beyond the commercial objectives of privately owned companies." Canada was committed to a "free market economy." This was a defining moment in China policy and broader economic policy from a government that had formerly eschewed economic nationalism and in a country that had a long and continuing experience with a variety of its own homegrown SOEs—more often known as Crown corporations— at least one of which, the Potash Corporation of Saskatchewan, had been spared from purchase by a private sector corporation three years earlier.

The limits and boundaries of "principled engagement" were becoming clearer. Public opinion does not determine policy, though it can constrain it. While the government was proceeding ahead with deeper commercial transactions, it was sensitive to critiques of China that included not just its behaviour but the core institution of its governance structure, the Chinese Communist Party.

This calculation of a fundamental conflict with China was not restricted to Conservatives. While Bob Rae, then interim leader of the Liberal Party, saw an invisible hand generated by economic interaction eventually transforming Chinese institutions and practices in a direction convergent with Canadian interests, other Liberals have taken a position closer to Preston Manning's. In the summer of 2012, Michael Ignatieff, a former leader of the Liberal Party, spoke in Riga about the "decisive encounter" between liberal democracies and post-Communist oligarchies in Russia and China "that have no ideology other than enrichment and are recalcitrant to global order," are "predatory on their own societies," and are "attempting to demonstrate a novel proposition that economic freedoms can be severed from political and civil freedom, and that freedom is divisible." He called for a "defiant stance toward the new tyrannies in China and Russia," framing them as "the chief strategic threat to the moral and political commitment of liberal democracies." But rather than seeing conflict as inevitable and eternal, he advocated responding with both curiosity and tolerance, avoiding the fixed categories of "us and them," "learning from beliefs we cannot share," and treating China as an opponent, not an enemy, while practising politics, not war or religion.[27]

The fear of a rising China has become greater than the sum of individual concerns. It is an exposed nerve. Public anxieties place limits on how deeply any Western government can embrace a China that is significantly different from it in values, history, and power. Conservative policy makers had initially reflected these concerns and then, after 2009, largely attempted to ignore or override them. But the very scale and dynamism of China's global presence and activities in Canada, especially in the area of investment, has made engagement far more complicated for both conservatives and liberal internationalists. The libertarian streak and prosperity agenda in Conservative Party thinking runs headlong into its deep antipathy to Communism; the engagement aspirations of liberal internationalism sit uneasily with the political philosophy of building a stronger human rights regime at home and abroad.

The moral case for engagement continues to be questioned by some who know China well. In a caustic account of Harper's 2012 visit to Beijing, Patrick Brown observed that no Canadian "has come up with a truly satisfactory answer to the challenge of doing business with a one-party state which is resolutely impervious to persuasion on human rights." Respect for human rights, he continued, is diminishing, with arbitrary arrests, disappearances, draconian sentences for expressing the slightest criticism, and lethal fire on demonstrators in Tibetan areas. The Communist Party ruthlessly defends its monopoly on power and protects the wealth amassed by its officials. "No matter how corrupt, greedy, and repressive China becomes, the only way forward appears to be engagement rather than isolation. But how to engage?"[28]

How to engage indeed.

chapter five

Engagement Recalibrated

China does not see itself as a rising, but as a returning power ... It does not view the prospect of a strong China exercising influence in economic, cultural, political, and military affairs as an unnatural challenge to world order—but rather as a return to a normal state of affairs.

Henry Kissinger, *On China*, 2nd ed. (2012), 546

Canada's China policy faces a complex set of choices that in scope, depth, and significance are second only to managing relations with the United States. Of frictions, abrasions, and opportunities, the issues *du jour*, there is no end. The relationship, however, needs to be judged in wider frame than the sum of its individual parts and the reactive management of individual pieces. Its long-term success depends on devising and articulating an overarching strategy that defines priorities and makes a compelling case why Canadians should support it.

Engagement is potentially more valuable at the same time that it is becoming more complicated in practice and more difficult to sell at home. The ambition to influence China, much less fundamentally change it, domestically or in its foreign relations, appears to some as quixotic, quaint, or delusional. Engagement is denounced by its critics as a fantasy, a twenty-first-century version of appeasement that has not produced significant change in China's political system or its human rights record. Despite deepening economic and human connections, the asymmetry of power is widening, and a rights-based Canada and an order-based China appear to be worlds apart. The challenge of being moral without being moralistic and resetting a moral compass at a time of shifting polarity is hard intellectually and complicated politically.

Aspirations and tactics from the past offer lessons and cautionary tales. The Canadian approach historically has been built on the idea that China is not a long-term enemy or threat. Sometimes that approach has reflected calculations of mutual interest, open-minded curiosity, mutual respect, self-confidence, and imagination. Sometimes it has reflected feelings of anger, superiority, self-righteousness, breathless adulation, and hypocrisy. Now, as then, the recurring theme is that Canadians seek a moral and strategic rationale beyond economic self-interest.

Canada will not determine the fate of China or the world in which China is a principal player. But it can reset and update its engagement strategy to be more comprehensive, ambitious, and imaginative. The aperture can be widened again to look at commercial relations and human flows not as ends in themselves but as part of a larger strategy of encouraging China's development as a constructive actor on the international stage. In large part this will depend on treating China for what it is and is becoming, irrespective of what we wish it to become. The task is not so much to change China in our own image as to adjust productively and peacefully to its evolution.

Recalibration can be based on four foundations: a clearer understanding of change in China and what it means; a new set of calculations about the nature of a multicentric world order and China's place in it; a strategic rather than transactional and mercantilist perspective; and national leadership to craft a next-generation Asia policy and communicate this to a concerned public.

Changing China

Few doubt that the social and economic development in China since recognition, especially since Deng Xiaoping's Open Door and reform policies of 1979, has been anything short of extraordinary.

In urban architecture, lifestyles, poverty reduction, rural migration to the cities, and the growth of religiosity, post-Deng China is a remarkable contrast to Mao's China. It is also vastly different from the China that Canadian missionaries knew in the first half of the twentieth century. Even in the face of extensive censorship and the great firewall, the information available to Chinese citizens about their country and the world is beyond the imagination of a generation ago.

For some Canadians the negativity about contemporary China focuses on social issues, including abortion, religious freedom, the one child policy, capital punishment, penal labour camps, labour policy and standards, product and food safety, environmental degradation, carbon dioxide emissions, and air- and water-borne pollution. For most, however, the concern is with the political system, corruption, rule by the Communist Party, limited respect for the basic political rights of free speech and assembly, and the absence of democratic elections that many Canadians see as good and a universal right. Moreover, polls by the Asia Pacific Foundation of Canada indicate that most Canadians perceive China to be regressing on human rights.

China indeed faces a veritable encyclopaedia of social ills, as if the problems of Charles Dickens's England or Lincoln Steffens's America during their great industrial revolutions are both magnified in scale and compressed in time. The serious problems of corruption, environmental degradation, sporadic violence, mass protests, and vast inequalities in contemporary China are not unfamiliar to observers of nineteenth-century Britain and early-twentieth-century America.

The hardest moral problem of engagement is defining expectations. If the only acceptable outcome is for China to embrace multiparty democracy and to understand and apply human rights as they have evolved in a Canadian context, China is bound to disappoint. If democracy and human rights are defined as categories with sharp boundaries, it will be easy to miss the micro-processes and developments already in motion.

The mistake is to paint China as static in either the problems it faces or the institutional responses to them. The Communist Party operates in many ways inconceivable in Mao's period. Its top leaders have fixed terms. A visit to the Central Party School is more like a visit to an executive MBA program than to a Marxist indoctrination centre. Multiple experiments with electoral mechanisms are underway at the county and provincial levels. And in many areas, including property rights, laws have been rewritten, judiciaries and the legal system improved, and, in some instances, rights spelled out in Chinese law and then upheld and enforced. A whole school of thought about deliberative democracy in China has emerged. Several provinces are eliminating the labour camps that have been in operation since the 1950s. The *hukou* system that severely limited internal migration and the one child policies have been relaxed. At the same time, censorship, repression, intimidation of critics of the regime, black jails, beatings, and detentions without trial continue.[1]

All of these developments are incomplete and zigzagging, like a game of snakes and ladders on a colossal scale. "The boulevard of freedoms that Chinese people may enjoy has widened," writes one veteran observer, "but it is still lined with precipices."[2] China remains an authoritarian system and is very unlikely to embrace Western-style multiparty democracy in the near future, if at all. Accordingly, for democratic fundamentalists, China is not a legitimate form of government, whatever the views of the majority of Chinese citizens.

If we look at China as a place and not a category, the trend line looks rather different. In an era of modular production and integrated supply and value chains, China is no longer about toys or textiles or the simple import of components, reassembly, and export. It is a global hub for high-tech manufacturing in sectors that include advanced electronics manufacturing, information technology, pharmaceuticals, and environmental technology and software. And it is bound deeply into the international financial system as the world's largest lender. This deep integration into the world economy may be the strongest agent of change.

Following this logic, Edward Steinfeld's *Playing Our Game: Why China's Rise Doesn't Threaten the West* argues that China's insertion into the international division of labour is reshaping its society and politics, not just its economy. Domestic laws and labour relations have been adjusted, and work units, lifetime employment, and free housing and health care all eliminated—a leap from Maoism to Reaganism in a single generation. To maintain its grip on power after June 4th, the Party leadership made the crucial decision to accelerate the move to a complete market economy defined in Western terms. This new social contract has proven popular even among those protesting against its distortions and inequities.

The political system remains arbitrary, opaque, and occasionally brutal, but it has produced what Steinfeld calls head-spinning change. A new kind of bureaucrat, often overseas-trained, is managing the economy. The country has been "transformed from a worn-out totalitarian throwback, a quirky and depressing historical outlier, to something far more recognizable, an authoritarian liberalizer in the East Asian development tradition." It is not just adopting values and institutions from the West, it is rapidly internalizing many of them, including law-based society, a focus on the individual citizen and protection of individual rights, mechanisms for accountability, and a long-term path to democratization. Neither an ally nor a friend, China is a partner "that shares with us an increasingly common set of values, practices, and outlooks … and an interest in sustaining the global system it has joined." It is fusing with the West, quickly—and largely on the West's terms.[3]

Even if overstated, this is good news for engagers. The invisible hand hinted at by Canadian leaders from Trudeau to Martin is not as invisible or ineffective as its critics contend. Economic self-interest is a powerful motivator. For China to be competitive and escape the middle-income trap, its trade and commercial laws will need to be strengthened in multiple areas, including intellectual property. As argued in a recent report commissioned by the Asia Pacific Foundation of Canada, it is at the intersection of where economic, social, and cultural rights meet civil and political rights that progress is most likely and important. Carefully implemented and part of an integrated strategy, Canadian trade and investment can support human rights through the protection of economic rights like safe labour conditions and social rights such as healthcare.[4]

Ottawa's focus going forward should be to encourage Chinese authorities to apply the principles of their own constitution and laws. The country's 1982 constitution outlined the value of a representative legislature, the right to ownership of private property, freedom of the press, and freedom of speech and assembly. The accountability China needs is accountability not to Western ideals and institutions but to the aspirations of its own people, who desire balanced growth, stability, personal security, and social harmony. As seen in the ASEAN's Declaration on Human Rights, China, like its Asian neighbours, is very likely to stress obligations as well as rights in implementing its own constitution.[5]

It no longer makes sense to talk about sanctions and withholding trade and investment as plausible instruments of policy. Sanctioning China in order to achieve particular political outcomes is no more feasible than imposing sanctions against the United States for its foreign policy or human rights failings.

The best means for promoting political rights remain the traditional Canadian formula of direct criticism and expressions of concern at the highest political level, quiet diplomacy in cases involving individuals, and an incessant effort at two-way dialogue, academic exchange, and capacity building. The bilateral and plurilateral dialogues were never more than just one instrument for discussion and were supplemented from the beginning by support for the training of jurists and lawyers; seminars and training courses on labour practice, minority rights, legislative drafting, and parliamentary exchanges; and high-level dialogue. Constructed properly, and used for genuine dialogue rather than denunciation and shaming, for making a difference rather than a point, they can address a range of critical issues.

Material and virtual connections to Chinese civil society have never been greater. Important instruments for promoting democratic development and human rights in China are a vast number of human connections, university exchange agreements, NGO collaborations, blogs, and websites—in short, day-to-day interactions on a thousand fronts. Professors, teachers, labour leaders, and students travelling in both directions can be at least as valuable as diplomats in building understanding and disseminating ideas. As Michael Ignatieff framed it after returning from his first trip to China, "Canadian politicians could hold press conferences on a daily basis to denounce the regime's shortcomings and still not accomplish what one visiting legal expert can by training Chinese judges."[6] Linking them to the embassy's new e-presence for public diplomacy, carefully handled, can open up a new frontier of engaging the Chinese public and not just the state.

In practical terms, CIDA has been the only large-scale instrument for funding and shaping these interactions. Imperfect as the bilateral program may have been, its termination in 2013 has left a major gap in leadership and funding for governance and other policy-related programs designed for dialogue and capacity building. While some—like the China Council for International Cooperation on Environment and Development, which has facilitated high-level policy exchange since its inception in 1992—will be continued through support from other Canadian ministries, many others will not. A new mechanism for funding bilateral cooperation and policy partnerships is essential.

Whose World Order?

A key part of the logic of engagement is that it has the capacity to alter China's international behaviour. This has been a staple in engagement thinking from Pierre Trudeau's effort to end the isolation of China, bring it into the international community, and reduce its dependence on the Soviet Union, to Paul Martin, Jr's idea of enmeshing China in a new set of international institutions in which it is a charter member.

Trying to influence an even more powerful China's view of the world may seem a real stretch. There are reasons to be modest about how much influence Canada has ever had on China's foreign affairs. Sceptics claim that not only has Canada's influence been minimal but that China is only interested in Canada insofar as it can give legitimacy to the Communist Party's efforts to strengthen its grip on power by being portrayed as a responsible international citizen. The argument may have had some validity immediately after Tiananmen Square, but China is now a major and self-confident player in almost every international organization.

With or without Canadian support, it will pursue its international role as norm taker, norm maker, and norm breaker according to its own national interests. The days when a visit by a foreign leader or China's entry into an international process was exciting domestic news in China have long since passed.

Canadians, like others, are divided in their estimates of what that international role is and is becoming. The projection of China as international outlier, supporter of odious regimes, assertive irredentist intent on recovering lost territory, and full-throttle challenger of a liberal international order misrepresents a much more complicated picture. China's participation in international institutions, like its domestic society, is evolving rather than static, uncharted rather than predestined. Disagreements with American and Canadian positions on current issues, ranging from North Korea to Syria and territorial conflicts in the western Pacific, are more the product of conflicting national interests and understandings of history than deep ideological differences.

As an international actor China is dramatically different than it was thirty years ago. It may have revisionist aspirations, but in its support for Westphalian norms of sovereignty it may be closer to the global mainstream than many Western nations. In most multilateral institutions, the Chinese are playing constructive roles—more or less "playing our game," if not with identical interests or perspectives. As a careful study by Rosemary Foot and Andrew Walter demonstrates, China is at least as likely as the United States to comply with international norms, in areas ranging from the use of force to financial regulation and climate change, if it has played a role in establishing them.[7] And even on sensitive matters related to sovereignty and non-interference in domestic affairs, there is fluidity in Chinese positions on issues like humanitarian intervention and the Responsibility to Protect. A decade ago China contested the doctrine on the basis of first principles. Now, it has largely agreed with Responsibility to Protect as a legitimate global concept, though it takes positions on its application based on its national interests and pragmatic calculations of its value in individual cases.

The questions, looking forward and as Chinese power increases, are: What will Chinese leaders want and think? Is there a reasonable chance of encouraging them to play either by "our" rules or by rules that we can help influence? Will it want per capita access to the global commons or live with a system where those who were there first get preferred access? For example, when calculating who will pay the major adjustment prices for slowing and mitigating climate change, will the price be paid by the countries whose past actions generated most of the problems or by those who are generating an increasing share of the problem now?

These are very complicated questions directed at a country that only very recently has had international responsibility thrust upon it and that remains primarily focused on its own domestic development. Did 1945 America know what role it would play in a post-Second World War international system? The complexity and lack of clear direction in Chinese thinking is seen in the proliferation of ideas in think tanks and universities, among journalists, and in government ministries and Party institutions.

Viewed in broader perspective, the key issue is not just China's rising power but whether its world view and applied theory will reproduce, converge with, or take a separate path from the world order and ideas produced in the era of trans-Atlantic dominance. When Canadian politicians speak of "fundamental differences" in values and systems, they are not just drawing categorical distinctions; they are often implying that the standards by which China should be judged are universal and defined in the West. Cultural and civilizational differences are unpopular and air-brushed out of the equation. "What we see when we compare West and East," wrote Christopher Patten, the last British governor of Hong Kong, "is a consequence more of time lags than of profound cultural differences."[8]

The best thinking by historians of China paints a more nuanced picture. John Fairbank and Wang Gungwu have in common the view that China cannot be expected to converge with or emulate American or Western-style modernity defined by type of political system and social values. When Chinese leaders speak of the universal values of human rights and democracy, they are in fact speaking a different language with a very different understanding of these values' meaning and forms. Cultural differences are deep and persistent even if they are incomplete and evolving. For a century and a half China has adapted to a state system and terms of international behaviour generated in the West while at the same time inheriting and taking forward long-standing patterns of Chinese centrality.

Where Fairbank emphasized interaction and accommodation,[9] Wang pays more attention to Chinese desires not merely to cope with outside pressures but to align with them. There is an undercurrent of both a Confucian identity and a cosmopolitan one. Wang makes the case for mutual respect in U.S.-China relations, "not because the Chinese now know how to behave like Americans, but because they are accepted as people who really want a peaceful environment for their country's development." China aims "to sustain civilized living and integrate modern ideas with the best of its own heritage."[10]

Wang also identifies a deep-rooted concept of change in the Chinese understanding of international affairs that is not based on an idea of progress and that sees all political orders as impermanent. "What China sees today is not an international order at all, least of all *the* international order," he argues, "but merely the product of the struggles among the Great Powers of half a century ago." The Cold War, bipolarity, and unipolarity are transient moments. The result is that China supports the existing international system, embodied in its role as a member of the P5 in the United Nations Security Council, but only for as long as suits its interests. It will support reform but only if it strengthens China's place in the world.[11]

Not just China's size but also its history of regional domination under the tributary system cause concern among its Asian neighbours in particular. China's regional critics fear the revival of Middle Kingdomism. Others are anxious about China as the purveyor of an alternative political and economic model—authoritarian capitalism. Sometimes referred to as the "Beijing consensus," it features the leadership role of the authoritarian party state, good governance rather than electoral democracy, technocratic approaches to government, an emphasis on social rights and obligations, reassertion of the principles of sovereignty and non-interference, and support for freer markets coupled with stronger regional and international institutions in which China plays a central role. This stands in contrast to a "Washington consensus" that features elected democracies, sanctity of individual political and civil rights, support for human rights, the promotion of free trade and open markets, and recognition of the doctrine of humanitarian intervention.

The fearful prospect of a Cold War-like ideological battle between China and the West is overstated. What distinguishes China from the Soviet Union is China's deep integration into market-based capitalism. Authoritarian capitalism and what Martin Jacques calls "the civilization state"[12] are powerful forces in China though unlikely to be reproduced or emulated elsewhere. They may change the world, but not in China's image. Only a few outside of China see its political system and ideology as attractive alternatives or believe it to be able to provide the public goods that its Asian neighbours or the world need.

The idea of competing visions of world order is overdrawn, yet it underscores that China is more inside than outside the world order as defined in Western terms. This can be cast as a Manichean confrontation of competing systems or, more constructively, as the zone of interaction between different starting points that both need to evolve. The American-inspired international system that took shape after the Second World War was never universal or uncontested. Even at its height, the Soviet Union, China, India, Indonesia, and many other parts of the world were not a part of it. China's current role is critical because it is the most powerful—though not the only—emerging player calling for new rules and possibilities.

For a China that itself was the upholder of its own universalism for two thousand years, far longer than America's exceptionalism, its international role and power put universalism on a new intellectual and political footing. If the current international order is the creation of dominant powers and is neither natural nor perfect, the questions of "Whose rules?" and "What principles?" become the defining issues in the building of international institutions, norms, and rules. The challenge is creating a rules-based international system with—rather than against—an equal power that often has different ideas and interests in defining what the rules should be.

If there is to be deeper convergence in future, it will be based on shared norms and common interests rather than imposed Western values and institutions. The search for shared rules, and the difficulty of finding them, is obvious on issues that range from the weaponization of space to humanitarian intervention, the definition and management of maritime boundaries, or the script for controlling cyber conflict. It becomes closely linked to interpretations of international law, treaties, and agreements and reappears in the definition of international standards in fields ranging from product safety to personalized medicine and genomic sequencing.

This puts Canada's middle-power role of the past in fresh perspective. The strategic outlook that China's leaders identified in Canada in 1970 included its capacity as a secure Western country to bridge at least some Cold War animosities between East and West. The contemporary middle-power role is bridging the differences between an established international order underpinned by the United States and the interests and ideas of a new set of emerging players, China chief among them. The G20 represents this ambition in one way, the BRICS group (Brazil, Russia, India, China, and South Africa) in another. In looking forward, our challenge is to find a way to ease a great power transition and foster rules, norms, and institutions that allow an ascending China and an established America to traverse a diagonal rather than crash into head-on conflict.

Operationally, this new middle-power role still involves getting China at as many tables as possible. It means extensive dialogue, capacity-building projects, and track-two and academic programs and exchanges. Those moments when Canada has made a difference, when the two sides have "clicked," have been built on right timing, open minds, and extensive, multi-tiered preparation. Philosophically, it means eschewing absolutes and searching for common ground. Operationally, it mean understanding and accommodating Chinese interests while attempting to place limits on them.

Geopolitics and Strategy

Conservative Ottawa has been particularly reluctant to address the geopolitical transition that has accelerated in the last ten years. This is perplexing considering that opinion polls show that Canadians perceive a major shift in China's influence relative to America's and have growing concerns about the quickening pace of Beijing's military modernization program. It is also curious considering that the overarching issue in Asia Pacific security is the rise of China and the implications this has for American military power and primacy. The drift of U.S.-China relations towards strategic rivalry and worry about unconstrained U.S.-China competition has animated discussion in regional institutions and national capitals for more than a decade, especially since the financial crisis of 2008, which underscored China's comparative and rising strength. The two suns in the Kepler sky circle each other with profound implications for the orbits of others in the system.

The Harper government has issued occasional statements on regional hotspots, including North Korea, where it has pursued a policy of "controlled engagement," regularly condemned North Korean actions, and joined the Proliferation Security Initiative designed to restrict the export of nuclear technology and fissile materials to and from North Korea. It has made general statements about developments in the South China Sea and other territorial disputes. And it has expanded its involvement in regional naval exercises and negotiated agreements for supply and services with Singapore and Japan in the event of regional emergencies on the western side of the Pacific. But it has been mute on China's defence modernization, the causes and implications of a deteriorating security situation in northeast Asia, China's interactions with its neighbours, America's pivot and rebalancing towards Asia, or the geopolitical interaction of the great powers, including China, the United States, Japan, India, and Russia.

Nor has the rekindled strategic partnership involved substantial discussion, much less high-level consultation, on multilateral institutions in an era of a rapidly shifting regional architecture. Since 2011, the Harper government has made a major push to accelerate bilateral free trade negotiations with several countries, joined the Trans-Pacific Partnership negotiations, and pressed for membership in the East Asia Summit process and the ASEAN Defence Ministers Meeting Plus process. It has signed several agreements with China connected to commercial relations and hinted at a future free trade agreement. But it has not provided an integrated rationale for these initiatives or connected them systematically to the strategic partnership with China—joint work on counterterrorism being one exception.

The contrast with policy discourse in our closest Asia Pacific allies is striking. The American "pivot" or "rebalancing" to Asia has been articulated at multiple levels by American officials, starting with President Obama. Its key elements are a reaction to rising Chinese power and the attempt to strike a balance between cooperation and competition in avoiding a headlong rush to rivalry and conflict. As America moved to shift the greater part of its military resources to Asia, Hillary Clinton summarized American policy as "attempting to work with a rising power to foster its rise as an active contributor to global security, stability and prosperity while also sustaining and securing American leadership in a changing world."[13]

Australia, Canada's most natural Asia Pacific comparator, is wrestling with the dilemma of having China as its largest trading partner and the United States as its principal security partner. The Australian discussion about China is intense, multidimensional, and features a vigorous public debate about the choices that Australia faces in response to China's rise in areas that include military defence and security. Its leaders have offered concrete proposals for building new multilateral mechanisms to deal with the strategic transition in the region. While serving as prime minister and foreign minister, Kevin Rudd championed the idea of an Asia Pacific Community including a Pax Pacifica to replace a Pax Americana and forestall a possible Pax Sinica. Another former prime minister, Paul Keating, has addressed the dangers of too heavy an accommodation with American foreign policy objectives and too much reliance on a "declining West." Analysts like Hugh White have highlighted a series of critical choices that Australia faces in light of U.S.-China tensions. In the event of a U.S.-China military clash over Taiwan, or a Japan-China clash over their maritime boundaries, where would Australia stand? What are the implications for Australia if the United States decides to resist China's rise, leave the region, or find a way to share power with China? A recent "White Paper on Australia in the Asian Century" gives a rationale and blueprint for a "whole-of-country" approach to Asia, and a 2013 Defence White Paper outlines a security and defence strategy premised on China's rise.[14] A contribution of $100 million from the federal government has assisted the Australian National University in establishing a major program on "China in the World" designed to deepen understanding and intellectual collaboration.

In Canada, save for a handful of academics and government officials, there has been little appetite for serious discussion of Asia Pacific security matters, China included. In the outpouring of recent writings and reports about Canada, Asia, and China the overwhelming emphasis has been on economic and commercial matters.[15] The reluctance to address geopolitics is also apparent in parliamentary circles. China commentary from the NDP and Bloc Québécois has for more than a decade focused almost entirely on human rights and trade. The strategic logic earlier enshrined in Liberal and Progressive Conservative thinking about engaging China, building multilateral institutions, bridging divides, and moderating great power competition is at least temporarily in hibernation. Canada's contemporary "security imaginary," to borrow Kim Nossal's term, denigrates geopolitics and has created a double feedback loop. Canadians tend not to respond to policy arguments framed in strategic terms, and very few politicians or leaders conceive of world politics in the hard language of geopolitics, in part because this has little resonance with the electorate.[16]

The consequences of this "a-strategic" approach are significant. Strategy matters to a China that has a comparatively stable leadership group and a special capacity for systematic, long-range planning, thinking, and action. Its Canada watchers frequently ask whether Canada now has a China strategy or a view of the world that extends beyond commerce and reflexive support for American policy. Others in Asia see Canada as a marginal, one-dimensional, and declining influence in a region where economics and security are closely intertwined.

Strategic clarity and vision matter even in pursuing a narrowly commercial agenda. A bilateral free trade agreement with China is the logical implication of the Complementarities Study concluded in 2012. To be sold to an anxious Canadian public it would have to be packaged as something larger than a strictly economic deal. While China, like Canada, negotiates on the basis of its economic interests, its free trade agreements are always connected to a political and strategic agenda. The Harper government's aspiration to become an energy superpower will depend upon capital from Asia and long-term supply agreements that will only be acceptable if they have both an environmental component and a strategic underpinning. Chinese investment in the Canadian energy sector and the prospect of trans-Pacific export of Canadian oil and gas to China have a significant geopolitical dimension. Long-term supply agreements and infrastructure investment depend upon there being a high level of confidence that today's trading partner will not become tomorrow's enemy.

In foreign policy, silence is preferable to a loud shout in the wrong direction. In general terms, the Canadian response to China's rise, its military build-up, and Sino-American competition can take one of three forms.

The first is a narrowly mercantilist approach in which Canada eschews significant involvement in the security affairs of China's immediate neighbourhood. Beyond a modest and largely symbolic role in non-traditional security issues, including counter-terrorism and illegal migration, the best course would be to focus on trade and investment opportunities and leave major defence obligations and decisions to the United States and its Asia Pacific allies. It would involve doing everything possible to avoid being caught in the middle of any military competition between the United States and China and stick to doing business with both.

The second is to deepen alliance relations with the United States, Australia, Japan, and, potentially, India and South Korea, in confronting China's rise, especially its expanding naval capabilities. Several proposals have been circulated for something alternatively called a league of democracies, an arc of democracies, an Asian NATO, or a D-10 to advance common democratic values and coordinate policies in containing China's expanding influence in Asia and globally. With the possible exception of Japan, this "Cold War Two" approach is not the mainline policy of any of these countries, though it does have instinctive appeal to some in government and policy communities in Canada for which values and the distinction between friends and enemies are paramount. It would involve major Canadian expenditures in an expanded naval presence in the region and deeper political collaborations with the like-minded in Asia and beyond.

The third is an integrated commitment to approaching Asian security issues through a significant increase in presence and funding for a combination of bilateral initiatives with China in military-to-military exchanges, dialogues, and track-two activities; renewed support for regional institutions and cooperative security arrangements in addressing a range of conventional and non-traditional security issues; and a diplomatic commitment to playing a balancing role in encouraging a positive outcome in U.S.-China relations.

As in Australia, a Canadian security strategy might well involve elements from all three, in the hope that the shift in power can be managed peacefully and constructively, and with a hedge towards cooperative defence if it cannot. But the options need to be openly discussed as part of a China-in-Asia policy. What precisely are the threats against which Canada should defend itself? What instruments are needed to respond to them—hard naval assets, missile defence systems, anti-terrorist capacity building, container security, multilateral diplomacy, intellectual and policy exchange?

Charting a strategic course also demands putting Asia and North America, including the United States, on a single map. While Canadian recognition of the PRC in 1970 produced expressions of concern in Washington, usually in the form of sadness rather than anger, the subsequent Canadian approach, when recognized at all, was more appreciated than condemned. Engagement became the core policy of U.S. presidents from Nixon to Obama, with only occasional wobbles. Congressional reactions have been more mixed, and there has been a chorus of responses against engagement and in support of cooler politics, cooler economics, and direct confrontation with China. Americans have tended to pay more attention to the strategic threat posed by China's rise even while focusing on the economic opportunities. Economically, trans-Pacific trade has put into focus the limitations of the North American Free Trade Agreement and has brought the United States, Canada, and Mexico into the Trans-Pacific Partnership Agreement negotiations. Canadian policy makers have been aware of American perspectives and interests and have largely followed in their wake, but on occasion have taken significantly different positions, including on missile defence options. A position "somewhat independent" of the United States remains valuable for Canada, the United States, and China.

National Leadership

When Marcel Masse made the case in the 1980s for the "multiplication of contacts at the thinking level," he could scarcely have guessed how complex the Canada-China relationship would be thirty years later. Seven different airlines fly non-stop each day between multiple locations in Canada and greater China. Hong Kong is now a special administrative region of the PRC and home to a quarter of a million Canadian citizens. More than a million and a quarter persons of Chinese descent live in Canada. Chinese languages—Mandarin and Cantonese combined—are the third most common in Canada. The "sinologist in residence" program in the Canadian Embassy in Beijing has terminated, but the number of professors teaching about China, researching China, or collaborating with Chinese partners has swelled. At the University of British Columbia alone there are more than two hundred professors with a significant professional interest in China and partnerships with more than ninety different institutions in greater China. There are now some 45,000 Chinese students studying at Canadian universities and colleges and at least 30,000 more in high schools and language schools. In addition to a small number of Canadian missionaries again operating in China, several thousand Canadians are teaching English in Greater China. There are well-functioning parliamentary exchanges through the Canada-China Legislative Association (currently with thirty senators and sixty MPs) and a host of ministerial and MP and senatorial visits to China each year. Provincial premiers and officials are frequent visitors. First Nations and virtually every major Canadian corporation have China strategies and contacts. Information about China and analysis of Chinese affairs is ubiquitous and provided by thousands of different sources, academics and government officials representing just one small sector. Media coverage of China is probably greater than that of any country in the world other than the United States.

At the same time, a drastically smaller number of Canadian students are studying at Chinese institutions or have co-op or internship placements in China, Taiwan, or Hong Kong. Few C-suite executives and senior officials and diplomats speak Chinese or another Asian language. According to the Asia Pacific Foundation of Canada studies, only about a quarter of Canadians feel that Asian languages, Chinese among them, should have more emphasis in our schools. There is a huge gap on many issues between the views of those who have extensive experience in and exposure to China and those who do not. A large number of backbench MPs and political staffers are unfamiliar with Asia. As the United States, Australia, Korea, Japan, and other countries ramp up their educational, societal, and governmental connections with China, Canada is lagging behind.

As tempting as it is to declare this the golden era in Canada-China relations and leave its future in the hands of enterprising citizens and organizations in China and Canada, government leadership remains essential. Whether by white paper, commission, or some other means, Canada needs an Asia strategy and a clearly articulated rationale and program for a major expansion of relations with China and its Asian neighbours.

Federal government leadership is fundamental, partly because the Chinese state is certain to remain a central actor in the Chinese economy and society for a very long time. It will be needed for regulatory purposes in managing an immensely more complicated agenda in areas including foreign investment, safety and inspections, and consular cases. It will be needed in outlining an approach to defence, security, trade, environmental protection, and investment.

Government leadership is needed to set ambitious goals, to generate resources for the kinds of policy exchanges that are beyond the capacity of the private sector and civil society, and to work with Canadians in thinking big. Government can convene stakeholders, offer incentives, and catalyse creative thinking. To get attention in

China, as in the United States, requires imagination and flair in occasionally making a big splash. Ministerial visits to China are easy and commonplace. Is it time for a meeting of Cabinet in China? What about an annual summit along the lines recently arranged by the Gillard government in Australia? How can we get more political staff and MPs to live in Asia? Why not establish a Conservative Party of Canada task force on the implications of the rise of Asia and the future of Canada-China relations?

If linking environment and energy is crucial to the sustainability of a long-term energy security equation for the two countries, why not establish a major joint centre? What about chairs of Canadian studies at major Chinese universities? What about setting a target for getting 10,000 Canadian students a year to China for experiential learning? How can we identify a next generation of Chinese leaders, some of them studying in Canada, and enrich their connections to policy and business networks across the country?

National leadership is also needed to refurbish and articulate the engagement narrative. China needs explaining. This in turn will depend upon an open policy process that again mobilizes intellectual talent and practical expertise to give us a chance at getting global China right. Politicians in every country—Canada, China, Australia, and the United States included—struggle to maintain domestic support for engagement strategies that are criticized by political opponents and that are viewed with suspicion by anxious publics. China needs careful understanding, and a China strategy needs to engage public opinions, not just reflect them.

There are hard choices ahead. What exactly are the aspects of Chinese SOEs and sovereign wealth funds that should cause concern? How can they be addressed? Is Chinese business practice likely to converge or collide with our own? Are our own North American variants of business practice indeed the gold standard or do they need adjustment, too? Are Chinese ambitions and practices in its naval deployment and cyber network exploitation fundamentally different from those of the United States and other great powers? When should we draw red lines in reacting to Chinese behaviour and ideas? When should we seek accommodation?

The chronicle of Canada-China relations reveals that there have always been good reasons for betting against China. Our missionaries encountered China at a moment of conflict, civil war, revolution, civil war, foreign invasion, poverty, weakness, and despair. The diplomats who aimed to recognize the new government of Mao Zedong in 1949 stuck to their belief that this was the right course even through a war with China in Korea. When the Diefenbaker government sold wheat to China, it was needed because of a Chinese famine induced by the Great Leap Forward. When Pierre Trudeau recognized the PRC in 1970 it was against the backdrop of the upheavals of the Cultural Revolution. When Paul Martin sealed the strategic partnership in 2005 there were voices that insisted that the Chinese economy could not sustain growth rates of 10 per cent per year—that the country was on the verge of implosion, large-scale and violent social protest, and potential war with Taiwan.

Yet the train of engagement thinking held that deepening political relations would benefit both countries and be a part of changing China and China changing the world has paid dividends on both sides. Even if engagement were an improbable bet, like Pascal's wager about believing in the existence of God, it is a good one. And forty years of close connections with China have coincided with developments that by any standards have been remarkably successful. China *is* moving in directions largely compatible with our interests and values, even if a perfect form of convergence his unlikely.

Canada's greatest long-term advantage may not be its diplomats, economic complementarity, energy and resources, human connections, or political and social values. It may be the Canadian sense of cosmopolitanism, the ability not to confuse our institutions with the perfect or the divine, our self-confidence that our own institutions and traditions prepare us well for the challenges of the twenty-first century, and the abiding belief that China is not "other" or an enemy but a different land with a different past and future that can be a partner and perhaps a *zhengyou*, even if not an ally. In a mature relationship, as Kevin Rudd has argued, when we agree, we should cooperate; when we disagree we should talk.

It will take wisdom, knowledge, and political courage to update the strategic partnership and recast the Canada-China narrative. Engagement with twenty-first-century characteristics demands eschewing absolutes and opening values and institutions, including our own, to constant interrogation and the search for common ground in a messy, multicentric world order that is shifting before our very eyes.

Notes

1 The China Policy Problem

1 David Shambaugh, *China Goes Global: The Partial Power* (New York: Oxford University Press, 2013), xi.
2 Interview with Richard Gorham, 16 February 1990.
3 Fred Bergsten, "A Partnership of Equals: How Washington Should Respond to China's Economic Challenge," *Foreign Affairs* (July/August 2008).
4 As explored in the essays in Alastair Iain Johnston and Robert S. Ross, eds, *Engaging China: The Management of an Emerging Power* (London: Routledge, 1999).
5 David Capie and Paul Evans, *The Asia-Pacific Security Lexicon*, 2nd ed. (Singapore: Institute of Southeast Asian Studies, 2008).

2 Trudeau to Tiananmen

1 Alvyn Austin, *Saving China: Canadian Missionaries in the Middle Kingdom, 1888–1959* (Toronto: University of Toronto Press, 1986).
2 Quoted in John English, "Lester Pearson and China," in Paul Evans and B. Michael Frolic, eds, *Reluctant Adversaries: Canada and the People's Republic of China 1949–1970* (Toronto: University of Toronto Press, 1991), 133.
3 Fred Edwards, "Chinese Shadows," in Robert Bothwell and Jean Daudelin, eds, *Canada among Nations, 2008: 100 Years of Canadian Foreign Policy* (Montreal: McGill-Queen's University Press, 2009), 296–7.
4 Brian Evans, *Pursuing China: Memoir of a Beaver Liaison Officer* (Edmonton: University of Alberta Press, 2012), 257–8.

5 Quoted in Peter Mitchell, "The Missionary Connection," in Frolic and Evans, *Reluctant Adversaries*, 30.

6 See Stephen Beecroft, "Canadian Policy toward China, 1949–1957: The Recognition Problem"; Norman St Amour, "Sino-Canadian Relations 1963–1968: The American Factor"; and Brian Evans, "Ronning and Recognition: Years of Frustration," in Evans and Frolic, *Reluctant Adversaries*.

7 John Diefenbaker, *Hansard*, 1 November 1957, 23rd Parliament, Session 1: 654. Hamilton's views are assessed in Patrick Kyba, "Alvin Hamilton and Canada-China Relations," in Frolic and Evans, *Reluctant Adversaries*.

8 Paul Evans and Daphne Taras, "Looking Far East: Parliament and Canada-China Relations, 1949–1982," in David Taras, ed., *Parliament and Canadian Foreign Policy* (Toronto: Canadian Institute of International Affairs, 1985).

9 The phrase "peaceful engagement" is attributed to R.L. Rogers and quoted by Fred Edwards in his "Chinese Shadows," in Bothwell and Daudelien, eds, *Canada among Nations, 2008*, 300.

10 Quoted in Beecroft, "Canadian Policy toward China," 68.

11 Don Page, "The Representation of China in the United Nations: Canadian Perspectives and Initiatives, 1949–1971," in Evans and Frolic, *Reluctant Adversaries*, 73–105.

12 John English, "Lester Pearson and China," in Evans and Frolic, *Reluctant Adversaries*, 133–48.

13 Paul Evans and Daphne Taras, "Canadian Public Opinion on Relations with China: An Analysis of the Existing Survey Research," Working Paper No. 33 (Toronto: Joint Centre on Modern East Asia, March 1985).

14 Jacques Hébert and Pierre Elliott Trudeau, *Two Innocents in Red China* (Toronto: Oxford University Press, 1968), 2.

15 Quoted in B. Michael Frolic, "The Trudeau Initiative," in Evans and Frolic, *Reluctant Adversaries*, 191.

16 Department of External Affairs, *Statements and Speeches*, No. 68/17 (28 May 1968).

17 Secretary of State for External Affairs, *Foreign Policy for Canadians* (Ottawa: Information Canada, 1970), 23–4.

18 Conversation with Trudeau, Montreal, 27 January 1987.

19 Department of External Affairs, "New Canadian Ties with China," *Statements and Speeches*, No. 73/21 (19 October 1973), 4.

20 Ivan Head and Pierre Elliott Trudeau, *The Canadian Way: Shaping Canada's Foreign Policy, 1968–1984* (Toronto: McClelland and Stewart, 1995), 123, 227, and 236–7. Italics added.

21 Bruce Gilley, "Reawakening Canada's China Policy," *Canadian Foreign Policy*, 114, 2 (Spring 2008): 122 and 121.

22 John English, *Citizen of the World: The Life of Pierre Elliott Trudeau, Volume One, 1919–1968* (Toronto: Knopf Canada, 2006), 350–6.

23 See Chen Wenzhao, "On the Uniqueness and Far-reaching Significance of the Establishment of Diplomatic Relations between China and Canada," and Mei Ping, "Remarks," both delivered at the workshop "Canada-China Relations: A Forty-Year Perspective," Shanghai, 10–12 November 2010. Available at: http://www.iar.ubc.ca/LinkClick.aspx?fileticket=w4g_qBv8tLM%3d&tabid=630. Accessed 10 June 2013.

24 Here and throughout this chapter and chapter 3 all of the Department of External Affairs quotations are from files in China 20-1-20 in the DFAIT archives.

25 Canadian International Development Agency, *China: Country Program Review, 1985–90* (December 1984) (Ottawa: CIDA, 1991).

26 All in DEA files, quoted in B. Michael Frolic, "Everybody Benefits: Canada's Decision to Establish a CIDA China Aid Programme in 1981." Conference paper presented at the Canadian Political Science Association, 4 June 1996.

27 *Independence and Internationalism*, Report of the Special Joint Committee of the Senate and House of Commons on Canada's International Relations (Ottawa: Supply and Services Canada, June 1986), 77.

28 Brian Mulroney, *Memoir: 1939–1993* (Toronto: McClelland and Stewart, 2007), 444–5.

29 As quoted and discussed in B. Michael Frolic, "Canada and China: The China Strategy of 1987," in Huhua Cao and Vivienne Poy, eds, *The China Challenge: Sino-Canadian Relations in the 21st Century* (Ottawa: University of Ottawa Press, 2011), 47–65.

30 Privy Council Office, Document 5-0096-87RD (01), 1 April 1987. Based on a Memo to Cabinet, 17 March 1987. Document 5-0096-87 MC (01).

31 B. Michael Frolic, "Six Observation about Sino-Canadian Relations since Tiananmen," Institute pierre renouvin, *Le Bulletin*, no. 10 (11 October 2000): 7.

3 Strategic Partnership

1 Joe Clark, House of Commons, *Hansard*, 5 June 1989.

2 Brian Mulroney, *Memoir: 1939–1993* (Toronto: McClelland and Stewart, 2007), 666.

3 Quoted in Fred Edwards, "Chinese Shadows," in Robert Bothwell and Jean Daudelin, eds, *Canada among Nations, 2008: 100 Years of Canadian Foreign Policy* (Montreal: McGill-Queen's University Press, 2009), 310.

4   Joe Clark, "China and Canada in the Months Ahead," Department of External Affairs, *Statements and Speeches*, 30 June 1989, 89/18: 2.

5   B. Michael Frolic, "The Beijing Massacre: A Canadian Perspective," paper presented at the Chinese University of Hong Kong (28 August 1989): 6; and "Myth and Reality: Rethinking China," *Globe and Mail*, 14 March 1992.

6   Interview, 16 February 1990.

7   Mulroney, *Memoir*, 849.

8   B. Michael Frolic, "Re-engaging China: Striking a Balance between Trade and Human Rights," in Fen Osler Hampson, Maureen Appel Molot, and Martin Rudner, eds, *Canada among Nations, 1997: Asia Pacific Face-Off* (Ottawa: Carleton University Press, 1997), 325.

9   Joe Clark, *Behind the Headlines*, 54, 1 (Fall 1996): 12.

10 Quoted in "A Change of Heart," *Maclean's*, 21 March 1994, and "Unusual Alliances," *Maclean's*, 22 May 1995.

11 Quoted in "Giving Trade Policy Black Marks: Proponents Say It's the Carrot, Not the Stick," *Toronto Star*, 19 May 1994.

12 DFAIT, Statement 94/25, 31 May 1994. See also Roy MacLaren, Statement 94/13, 29 March 1994, 1–4.

13 "Canada Can't Sway China on Rights, PM Says," *Globe and Mail*, 19 March 1994.

14 David Van Praagh, "China's Real Agenda," *Globe and Mail*, 30 June 1998.

15 Lloyd Axworthy, *Navigating a New World: Canada's Global Future* (Toronto: Knopf Canada, 2002), 57.

16 Charles Burton, "Assessment of the Canada-China Bilateral Human Rights Dialogue," DFAIT, 19 April 2006.

17 *Globe and Mail*, 19 March 1994; and "PM Confident Asia Tour Will Help Human Rights," *Toronto Star*, 18 November 1994.

18 House of Commons, *Hansard*, 4 June 1996.

19 Susan Shirk, *China: The Fragile Superpower* (New York: Oxford University Press, 2007), 118.

20 Jeremy Paltiel, "Canada in China's Grand Strategy," *China Papers*, No. 6, Canadian International Council, January 2010: 8–9.

21 "Time to Take a Bold Step toward China," *Globe and Mail*, 17 January 2005.

22 Address to the Canada-China Business Council, Beijing, 21 January 2005.

23 "China, Canada Agree to Establish Strategic Partnership," *China View* (published by Xinhua on line), 11 September 2005.

24 Bill Graham, "The Future of Canada-China Relations," speech to the conference "Canada-China Relations: An Evaluation," University of

Toronto, 23 April 2004. Portions are reprinted in the *CANCAPS Bulletin*, No. 41 (May 2004): 10–12.

25 DFAIT, News Release, "Canada Announces Funding for Human Rights Project in China," February 2005.

26 Thomas Axworthy, "Don't Let Ideals Devour Democracy," *Globe and Mail*, October 2004; and "Economic Doomsday Looms for China's Rulers," and "Engage but Don't Kowtow," *Toronto Star*, 24 and 25 July 2005.

27 Stanley Hartt, "Must We Choose between Trade and Human Rights?" *Globe and Mail*, 20 January 2005.

28 *Globe and Mail*, 23 October 2004 and 29 October 2005.

29 Geoffrey York, "China Knows How to Dance with Canada on Human Rights," *Globe and Mail*, 22 January 2005; *Winnipeg Free Press*, 12 September 2005.

30 Stockwell Day, "Canada Must Work for Global Democracy," *Toronto Star* (Ontario Edition), 10 April 2003; quoted in "China Favours Peaceful Solution to Taiwan Trouble, Premier Says," *Ottawa Citizen*, 12 December 2003; *Hansard*, no. 150, 38th Parliament, 1st Session, 15 November 2005.

31 Quoted in Lloyd Mackay, *The Pilgrimage of Stephen Harper* (Toronto: ECW Press, 2005), 169–70.

32 Stephen Harper, "Challenges and Moral Guidance: Freedom of Religion Has Come under Attack," *Ottawa Citizen*, 12 January 2006: A.15.

33 Jason Kenney, Press Release, 8 January 2005.

4 Harper's Turn

1 Conservative Party of Canada, *Stand Up for Canada: Federal Election Platform*, January 2006: 44. Available at: http://www.cbc.ca/canadavotes2006/leadersparties/pdf/conservative_platform20060113.pdf.

2 Roy Rempel, *Dreamland: How Canada's Pretend Foreign Policy Has Undermined Sovereignty* (Montreal and Kingston: McGill-Queen's University Press, 2006).

3 See Brian Laghi, "China Snubs Harper," *Globe and Mail*, 15 November 2006; John Geddes and Jason Kirby, "The China Dilemma," Macleans. ca, 27 November 2006; Charlie Gillis, "Touching Off Our China Crisis," *Maclean's*, 4 December 2006.

4 *Interview with Jason Kenney*, Question Period-CTV, 6 December 2009.

5 The view is attributed to David Emerson by Lawrence Martin in *Harperland: The Politics of Control* (Toronto: Viking Canada, 2010), 83.

6 "China 'Worst Human Rights Abuser in the World': Tory MP," CBC News, 17 April 2008.

7   Canada-China Legislative Association "report." Available at: http://
www.parl.gc.ca/IIAPublications/Document.aspx?sbdid=cb334500-91cd-
413e-8afb-254fd29e182a&sbpidx=1&Language=E&Mode=1&sbpid=8d
5d26d4-ab73-4716-8274-f453865e5730.

8   "China Lashes Out: A Chinese Official Takes Aim at Canadian Criticisms
of His Country's Human Rights Record," *Maclean's*, 9 February 2007.
Available at: http://www.macleans.ca/article.jsp?content=20070209
_122747_9272.

9   Alan Freeman and Geoffrey York, "Sino-Canadian Relations Dealt
Severe Blow," *Globe and Mail*, 9 November 2007.

10   Quoted in Campbell Clark, "Personal Financial Interest behind Chrétien
Attack on PM's China Policy, Kenney Says," *Globe and Mail*, 20 August 2008.

11   John Ivison, "Signs Hint of a New Approach to Chinese Relations,"
National Post, 27 September 2007.

12   Stephen Harper, speech in Shanghai, 4 December 2009.

13   John Ibbitson, "A New Era for Canada Rises in the East," *Globe and Mail*,
8 December 2009.

14   Baird speech to the Canada-China Business Council, in Toronto, 29 June
2011.

15   Campbell Clark and Mark Hume, "Baird Embraces China as a 'Friend,' "
Globe and Mail, 19 July 2011; and Rod Mickelburgh, "Coincidence? Lai
Decision Comes as Baird off to Beijing," *Globe and Mail*, 15 July 2011.

16   Stephen Harper, Guangzhou dinner speech, 10 February 2012.

17   Quoted in Andy Hoffman, "Canada-China Ties 'Very Warm,' Envoy
Says," *Globe and Mail*, 30 August 2011.

18   Quoted in Patrick Brown, "Harper in China: Great, Glorious and Always
Correct," 9 February 2012, Global News blog, Available at: http://
globalnews.ca/national/program/global-national/?id=6442577027&
blogid=6442450996.

19   Paul Evans and Daphne Taras, "Canadian Public Opinion on Relations
with China: An Analysis of the Existing Survey Research," Working
Paper No. 33 (Toronto: Joint Centre on Modern East Asia, March 1985).

20   The Asia Pacific Foundation of Canada has conducted annual national
opinion polls on Canadian views of Asia, China included, since 2004,
and all are available on its website at: http://www.asiapacific.ca/sur-
veys/national-opinion-polls. The most recent was released in May 2013
and can be accessed at: http://www.asiapacific.ca/surveys/national-
opinion-polls/2013-national-opinion-poll-canadian-views-asia.

21   David Ljunggren, "Tory MP Slams CNOOC Takeover Bid for Nexen,"
National Post, 7 November 2012.

22 David Matas and David Kilgour, "Calling China to Account," *Globe and Mail Update*, 30 May 2008.
23 Lawrence Solomon, "Harper's Mission," *Financial Post*, 3 February 2012.
24 Terence Corcoran, "Panda Politics: It's Trickier Than You Think," *Financial Post*, 10 February 2012; Terry Glavin, "Defenceless," *Ottawa Citizen*, 4 February 2012; and Andrew Cohen, "Canada Sells Out to China," *Ottawa Citizen*, 14 February 2012.
25 Preston Manning, "Use Principles, Not Mere Pragmatism," *Globe and Mail*, 21 November 2012.
26 David Mulroney, "There's No Shortcut to China," *Globe and Mail*, 6 November 2012.
27 Michael Ignatieff, "How Should Liberal Democracies Deal with China and Russia?" Isaiah Berlin Riga Memorial Lecture, June 2012. Available at: http://blogs.reuters.com/great-debate/2012/07/12/how-should-liberal-democracies-deal-with-china-and-russia/.
28 Patrick Brown, "Harper in China."

5 Engagement Recalibrated

1 A balanced assessment reflecting the Canadian experience is Chantal Meagher, "China's Fifth Modernization: The Enduring Hope for Democratic Governance," *A Diplomat's Handbook for Democracy Development Support*, 2011: http://www.diplomatshandbook.org/.
2 Peter Ford, "Amid Human Rights Protests: A Look at China's Record," *Christian Science Monitor*, 10 April 2008: http://www.csmonitor.com/World/Asia-Pacific/2008/0410/p04s01-woap.html.
3 Edward S. Steinfeld, *Playing Our Game: Why China's Rise Doesn't Threaten the West* (Oxford: Oxford University Press, 2010), 115 and 233.
4 Pitman Potter, Sharon Hom, Douglas Horswill, Joseph Ingram, and Robert Wright, "Advancing Canada's Engagement with Asia on Human Rights," Asia Pacific Foundation of Canada, 25 September 2013. Available at http://www.asiapacific.ca/research-report/advancing-canadas-engagement-asia-human-rights.
5 ASEAN Human Rights Declaration, 19 November 2012: http://www.asean.org/news/asean-statement-communiques/item/asean-human-rights-declaration.
6 Michael Ignatieff, "Raising Our Game in Canada-China Relations," *Policy Options* (September 2010): 7.
7 Rosemary Foot and Andrew Walter, *China, the United States and Global Order* (Cambridge: Cambridge University Press, 2011).

8   Christopher Patten, *East and West: China, Power and the Future of East Asia* (London: Times Books, 1998), 166.

9   John K. Fairbank, *The United States and China*, 4th rev. and enlarged ed. (Cambridge, MA: Harvard University Press, 1983), 477; *The Great Chinese Revolution, 1800–1985* (New York: Harper and Row, 1986); "China's Foreign Policy in Historical Perspective," originally published in *Foreign Affairs* (April 1969) and republished in his collection of essays, *China Perceived: Images and Policies in Chinese-American Relations* (New York: Alfred A. Knopf, 1975).

10   Wang Gungwu, *Joining the Modern World: Inside and Outside China* (Singapore: Singapore University Press, 2000), 108 and 126; and "China Rises Again," *Yale Global* (25 March 2009): 4.

11   Wang Gungwu, "China and the International Order: Some Historical Perspectives," in Wang Gungwu and Zheng Yongnian, eds, *China and the New International Order* (London and New York: Routledge, 2008), 22 and 26.

12   Martin Jacques, *When China Rules the World*, 2nd ed. (London: Penguin Books, 2012), ch. 7.

13   Hillary Clinton, "Remarks at the U.S. Institute of Peace China Conference," Washington, D.C., 7 March 2012: http://www.state.gov/secretary/rm/2012/03/185402.htm.

14   Kevin Rudd, "The Prospects for Peace in the Pacific: The Future of the Expanded East Asia Summit," speech to the Asia Society, New York, 13 January 2012: http://asiasociety.org/policy/strategic-challenges/intra-asia/complete-text-australian-foreign-minister-kevin-rudds-speech-; Paul Keating, "Why America Cannot Ignore the China Choice," *East Asia Forum*, 8 August 2012; Hugh White, *The China Choice: Why America Should Share Power* (Collingwood: Black Inc., 2012); Australia in the Asian Century White Paper, 2012: http://pandora.nla.gov.au/pan/133850/20130914-0122/asiancentury.dpmc.gov.au/white-paper.html; Government of Australia, Department of Defence, Defence White Paper 2013: http://www.defence.gov.au/whitepaper2013/docs/WP_2013_web.pdf.

15   Among them Wendy Dobson, "Canada, China, and Rising Asia: A Strategic Proposal," paper published by the Canada-China Business Council and the Canadian Council of Chief Executives, 2012: http://www.ceocouncil.ca/wp-content/uploads/2011/10/Strategic-proposal-ENGLISH-25-oct-low-resolution.pdf; and Derek Burney, Fen Hampson, and Leonard Edwards, "Winning in a Changing World: Canada and Emerging Markets," *iPolitics*, 2012: http://m.gowlings.com/knowledgecentre/publicationPDFs/20120626_Winning-in-a-Changing-World-EN.pdf. An

exception that links economic and security issues is Donald Campbell, Paul Evans, and Pierre Lortie, "Securing Canada's Place in Asia: Means, Institutions and Mechanisms," Asia Pacific Foundation of Canada, 6 September 2012: http://www.asiapacific.ca/research-report/securing-canadas-place-asia-means-institutions-and-mechanism.

16 Kim Nossal, "An 'A-Strategic' Power: Canada, China and Great Power Transition," in James Ferguson, ed., *Essays in Honour of Paul Buteux* (Vancouver: University of British Columbia Press, forthcoming 2014).

Index